10 Ways to Avoid Probate

Steven M. Bragg

AccountingTools®

Published by AccountingTools, Inc., Centennial, Colorado.

ISBN-13: 978-1-64221-351-5

For more information about AccountingTools® products, visit our Web site at www.accountingtools.com.

Table of Contents

About the Author

Steven Bragg, CPA, has been the chief financial officer or controller of four companies, as well as a consulting manager at Ernst & Young. He received a master's degree in finance from Bentley College, an MBA from Babson College, and a Bachelor's degree in Economics from the University of Maine. He has been a two-time president of the Colorado Mountain Club, and is an avid alpine skier, mountain biker, and certified master diver. Mr. Bragg resides in Centennial, Colorado. He has written more than 300 books and courses, including *New Controller Guidebook*, *GAAP Guidebook*, and *Payroll Management*. He has also written *The Auditors* science fiction trilogy.

Steven maintains the accountingtools.com web site, which contains continuing professional education courses, the Accounting Best Practices podcast, and thousands of articles on accounting subjects.

How to Avoid Probate

Introduction

This course explains why probate can be costly, slow, and intrusive, and why many individuals seek to structure their affairs to avoid it. It introduces the legal and practical foundations of probate, and then examines how ownership, beneficiary designations, and contractual transfers determine whether court involvement is required at death. The course walks through ten commonly used probate-avoidance strategies, explaining how each one works, when it is effective, and where it can create unintended risks if used incorrectly. The objective is to provide a practical framework for evaluating probate-avoidance tools and coordinating them into a coherent estate plan.

What is Probate?

Probate is the court-supervised legal process used to settle a deceased person's estate. Its purpose is to validate the decedent's will, if one exists, identify and inventory assets, pay outstanding debts and taxes, and distribute any remaining property to heirs or beneficiaries. If there is no will, probate also determines who is legally entitled to inherit under state intestacy laws. During probate, the court appoints a personal representative, often called an executor or administrator, who has fiduciary responsibility for managing estate assets and carrying out required procedures. Probate provides a formal structure that protects creditors and beneficiaries by ensuring transparency and oversight, but it can also be time-consuming and costly.

Why We Want to Avoid Probate

Many people seek to avoid probate because it can impose significant administrative, financial, and personal burdens on an estate and its beneficiaries. Probate is often slow, with statutory waiting periods and court schedules that can delay access to assets for months or even years. The process can also be expensive, involving court costs, executor fees, attorney fees, and appraisal expenses that reduce the value of the estate. In addition, probate proceedings are generally public, meaning that details about assets, debts, and beneficiaries become part of the public record, which can undermine family privacy. Probate also introduces rigidity, since distributions must follow court procedures rather than the practical needs of heirs. For families facing immediate cash needs, these delays can be particularly disruptive. Probate also becomes more complex when assets are located in multiple states, potentially triggering multiple probate proceedings. Finally, probate increases the risk of disputes, as formal notice requirements and public filings can invite will contests or creditor claims. By avoiding probate, an estate can be settled more efficiently, privately, and with greater control over timing and outcomes.

Option 1: The Revocable Living Trust

A revocable living trust is one of the most widely used estate planning tools for individuals who want to avoid probate while retaining full control over their assets during their lifetime. Its effectiveness lies not in avoiding legal ownership, but in changing how ownership is structured and administered at death. Probate is required when assets are owned in an individual's name at death with no contractual or trust-based mechanism to transfer them. A properly created and funded revocable living trust shifts that transfer process outside the probate system by ensuring that assets are already held under a continuing legal entity that does not cease to exist at death.

A revocable living trust works by changing the ownership structure of assets during the grantor's lifetime. The person who creates the trust, often called the grantor or settlor, establishes a legal trust agreement and transfers assets into the trust. In most cases, the grantor also serves as the initial trustee and the primary beneficiary during life. This arrangement allows the grantor to maintain the same practical control over assets as before. The trust can be amended, restated, or revoked entirely at any time while the grantor is competent. Because of this retained control, the trust does not provide creditor protection or tax sheltering during life, but that is not its primary purpose.

The key probate-avoidance feature of a revocable living trust is the continuity of ownership. When an individual dies, property titled in that individual's name becomes subject to probate because the owner no longer exists as a legal person capable of holding title. A trust, however, does not die. The trust continues to exist after the grantor's death, and the successor trustee named in the trust document automatically steps into authority without court appointment. Because the trust already owns the assets, there is no need for a court to transfer title from a deceased person to heirs.

EXAMPLE

Maria Lopez is a retired teacher who owns a home, brokerage account, and savings account titled in the name of the Maria Lopez Revocable Living Trust. During her lifetime, Maria serves as both grantor and trustee, managing the assets as if she owned them outright. When Maria dies, she does not legally own the trust assets, because the trust does. The successor trustee named in the trust document immediately assumes control without court involvement. The trustee can pay expenses and distribute property to beneficiaries according to the trust terms. Because no assets are titled in Maria's individual name, probate is not required to transfer ownership.

Funding the trust is essential to achieving probate avoidance. Creating a trust document alone does not avoid probate if assets remain titled in the individual's personal name. Real estate must be retitled into the name of the trust by deed. Bank and brokerage accounts must be retitled or otherwise formally transferred to the trust. Business interests, investment accounts, and non-qualified assets must also be properly assigned. Assets that are not transferred into the trust remain subject to probate unless they pass by beneficiary designation or joint ownership. Many probate problems arise not from defective trust documents but from incomplete or inconsistent funding.

Once assets are titled in the trust, the grantor continues to use them as before. Income generated by trust assets is typically reported under the grantor's Social Security number during life, so there is no change in income tax reporting. The grantor can buy, sell, refinance, or reinvest trust assets freely. From a functional standpoint, the trust is largely invisible during life. This invisibility is often misunderstood, leading some people to underestimate the trust's importance. The benefit appears only at death or incapacity, when the trust's administrative structure becomes critical.

At death, the successor trustee assumes responsibility for administering the trust according to its terms. This transition does not require probate court approval. The successor trustee typically provides notice to beneficiaries and creditors as required by state law, marshals trust assets, pays valid debts and expenses, and distributes property to beneficiaries. All of this occurs privately, without court supervision unless a dispute arises. The absence of mandatory court involvement is what allows the trust to avoid probate.

EXAMPLE

When Daniel Chen dies, his revocable living trust names his sister, Laura Chen, as successor trustee. Upon his death, Laura immediately assumes authority without seeking probate court approval. She notifies beneficiaries and creditors as required by state law, gathers Daniel's trust assets, and pays outstanding bills and final expenses from the trust. She then follows the trust's written instructions to distribute assets to Daniel's children. Throughout the process, no court filings or hearings are required, and the administration remains private. Only if a beneficiary challenges Laura's actions would a court become involved. This streamlined transition is what allows Daniel's trust to avoid probate entirely.

Another important probate-avoidance function of a revocable living trust involves incapacity planning. Probate avoidance is not limited to death. If an individual becomes incapacitated without a trust, a court-supervised conservatorship or guardianship may be required to manage assets. A revocable living trust allows the successor trustee to step in upon incapacity, using standards defined in the trust document. This continuity further reinforces the trust's role as an alternative to court oversight, both during life and at death.

Privacy is a significant benefit closely tied to probate avoidance. Probate proceedings are public records. Wills, asset inventories, creditor claims, and beneficiary distributions may be accessible to anyone willing to search court records. A revocable living trust, by contrast, is a private document. Trust administration occurs outside the public court system, and details of the estate remain confidential among the trustee, beneficiaries, and advisors. This privacy can reduce family conflict and protect beneficiaries from unwanted attention.

The trust also simplifies administration for estates that include real estate in multiple states. Without a trust, real estate located outside the decedent's home state typically requires ancillary probate in each additional state. This can be costly and time-consuming. When real estate is titled in a revocable living trust, a single successor trustee can administer all properties without opening separate probate cases. Deeds can be transferred or properties sold under the trustee's authority, eliminating jurisdictional complications.

Revocable living trusts also allow for more efficient timing of distributions. Probate courts often impose mandatory waiting periods for creditor claims and may delay distributions until the court approves final accountings. Trust administration can proceed on a more flexible timeline, subject to statutory notice requirements and prudent administration standards. This flexibility can be especially important when beneficiaries need timely access to funds for living expenses, education, or debt obligations.

Does a Revocable Living Trust Avoid Taxes?

It is important to distinguish probate avoidance from tax avoidance. A revocable living trust does not, by itself, reduce estate taxes or income taxes. For tax purposes, assets in a revocable trust are treated as owned by the grantor during life and included in the grantor's taxable estate at death. However, the trust structure provides a platform for incorporating tax planning provisions, such as credit shelter trusts or marital trusts, that become effective at death without probate. The trust serves as a container for those strategies, even though it does not create tax savings on its own.

A common misconception is that a will alone can avoid probate if it is simple or uncontested. In reality, a will is a probate instrument. Its primary function is to direct the probate court on how assets should be distributed. A revocable living trust operates independently of the probate court, which is why it is effective in avoiding probate. In many estate plans, a will still exists alongside the trust, often called a pour-over will[1]. This will directs any assets left outside the trust at death to be transferred into the trust through probate. While this does not eliminate probate entirely, it minimizes its scope and ensures consistency in asset distribution.

Tip: The success of a revocable living trust in avoiding probate depends heavily on ongoing maintenance. Assets acquired after the trust is created must be titled in the trust or designated to pass into it. Changes in financial institutions, property refinancings, or business restructurings can inadvertently remove assets from the trust. Regular review is necessary to ensure that the trust remains fully funded and aligned with the individual's asset profile.

From an administrative standpoint, trust-based estate settlement is often less burdensome for family members. The successor trustee is guided by the trust document rather than by court orders. Professional trustees or advisors can be engaged without court approval. Beneficiaries often experience fewer procedural delays and lower

[1] A pour-over will is a will that directs any assets remaining in a person's individual name at death to be transferred into an existing revocable living trust, ensuring that those assets are ultimately distributed according to the trust's terms.

administrative costs. While trustee fees may apply, these are often comparable to or lower than combined probate costs, especially in states with statutory probate fee schedules.

The trust's flexibility also allows for tailored distribution provisions that function smoothly without probate oversight. Staggered distributions, continuing trusts for minors, asset protection provisions for beneficiaries, and special needs planning can all be administered privately through the trust structure. Probate courts can implement similar provisions, but doing so typically involves ongoing court supervision, reporting requirements, and potential delays.

It is also worth noting that probate avoidance does not mean the absence of legal accountability. Trustees are fiduciaries and are legally obligated to act in the best interests of beneficiaries. Beneficiaries retain the right to receive information and to challenge trustee actions if misconduct occurs. The difference is that court involvement is reactive rather than mandatory. This shift reduces administrative friction while preserving legal protections.

In practical terms, a revocable living trust transforms estate settlement from a court-driven process into a privately administered one. Assets do not change ownership at death because they are already owned by the trust. Authority does not need to be granted by a judge because it is granted by the trust document itself. Distribution does not require court approval because the trustee acts under fiduciary law rather than probate law. Each of these structural changes contributes to probate avoidance.

For individuals with significant assets, blended families, business interests, or privacy concerns, the advantages of probate avoidance can be substantial. Even for more modest estates, the predictability and efficiency of trust administration often justify the upfront effort of creating and funding the trust. The true value of a revocable living trust is revealed not during the grantor's lifetime, when it appears largely inert, but at the moment when probate would otherwise be triggered.

Option 2: Joint Ownership with Right of Survivorship

Joint ownership with right of survivorship has long been used as a practical estate planning tool to avoid probate, particularly for individuals who prefer simplicity, privacy, and continuity of ownership at death. At its core, this form of ownership allows property to pass automatically to the surviving owner or owners upon the death of one joint owner, without the need for court involvement. The effectiveness of this mechanism lies not in elaborate legal maneuvering, but in the way property law defines ownership interests during life and reallocates those interests at death. Understanding how and why this works requires an examination of the legal nature of joint ownership and the practical consequences of using survivorship rights as a substitute for testamentary transfers.

The legal foundation of joint ownership with right of survivorship is the concept that each owner holds an undivided interest in the entire property, rather than a divisible fractional share that can be transferred at death. When one owner dies, that person's interest does not pass to heirs or beneficiaries. Instead, it is extinguished, and the surviving owner's interest expands by operation of law to encompass full ownership.

Because no transfer occurs at death in the traditional sense, there is nothing for the probate court to administer with respect to that property. Ownership simply continues in the hands of the survivor.

This structure contrasts sharply with property held solely in the decedent's name. Sole ownership creates a distinct ownership interest that must be transferred upon death, either under a will or under intestacy laws if no will exists. That transfer requires probate because the court must confirm the validity of the will, appoint a representative, and authorize the distribution of assets. Joint ownership with right of survivorship bypasses these steps by ensuring that the decedent's interest never becomes part of the probate estate in the first place.

In practical terms, the most common forms of joint ownership with right of survivorship include joint tenancy with right of survivorship for real property, joint bank accounts, and certain forms of jointly titled investment accounts. In many jurisdictions, spouses also have access to specialized forms of ownership such as tenancy by the entirety, which includes survivorship rights and additional creditor protections. While the terminology and default rules vary by state, the essential feature is the same: survivorship overrides testamentary intent and operates automatically at death.

What is Tenancy by the Entirety?

Tenancy by the entirety is a form of joint property ownership available only to married couples in certain states, where each spouse is considered to own the entire property rather than a divisible share. Upon the death of one spouse, the surviving spouse automatically becomes the sole owner by operation of law, and the property is generally protected from the individual creditors of either spouse.

The probate-avoidance benefit of survivorship ownership is especially apparent in the context of real estate. Real property often represents a significant portion of an individual's wealth, and transferring title through probate can be slow and expensive. When a home is owned jointly with right of survivorship, the surviving owner typically needs only to record a death certificate or an affidavit of survivorship with the local land records office. Once recorded, title is clear, and the survivor can sell, refinance, or otherwise deal with the property without waiting for probate proceedings to conclude. This immediate clarity of ownership can be critical for maintaining housing stability or meeting financial obligations tied to the property.

EXAMPLE

When Margaret Wilson purchased her home in Arizona, she titled it jointly with her husband, Robert Wilson, as joint tenants with right of survivorship. Years later, when Robert died unexpectedly, Margaret faced an emotionally difficult period but avoided an additional legal burden. Instead of hiring an attorney and opening a probate estate just to transfer title to the home, Margaret obtained several certified copies of Robert's death certificate. She recorded one copy, along with a simple affidavit of survivorship, with the county recorder's office. Within days, the public records reflected her as the sole owner of the property. This clarity allowed Margaret to refinance the mortgage to reduce monthly payments and later sell the home when she decided to downsize. At no point did she need court approval to act. The survivorship feature ensured that ownership passed automatically, allowing Margaret to focus on stabilizing her finances and planning her next steps without delay or unnecessary expense.

Joint bank accounts operate in a similar manner. Upon the death of one account holder, the surviving owner retains full access to the account. Funds are not frozen pending probate, and there is no requirement to obtain court approval before using the money. This liquidity can be particularly important in the period immediately following a death, when funeral expenses, medical bills, and ongoing household costs must be paid. By contrast, accounts titled solely in the decedent's name may be inaccessible until a personal representative is appointed and authorized to act.

Another advantage of avoiding probate through joint ownership is privacy. Probate proceedings are generally matters of public record. Wills, inventories of assets, and accountings of distributions may be accessible to anyone willing to review court files. Jointly owned property that passes by survivorship does not appear in probate filings, shielding both the existence of the asset and its value from public view. For individuals who value confidentiality in financial and family matters, this aspect of survivorship ownership can be a compelling benefit.

The simplicity of survivorship transfers also reduces administrative costs. Probate often involves court filing fees, attorney fees, appraisal costs, and executor commissions. While the exact amounts vary by jurisdiction and estate size, these expenses can meaningfully reduce the value of an estate. Assets that pass outside probate through joint ownership are not subject to these costs, allowing the survivor to retain the full value of the property. For modest estates in particular, the cost savings can be disproportionate to the complexity of the planning required to achieve them.

Despite these advantages, the use of joint ownership with right of survivorship as a probate-avoidance strategy is not without trade-offs. One important consequence is the loss of control over the ultimate disposition of the property. Because survivorship rights override a will, the original owner cannot direct the property to anyone other than the surviving joint owner. This may be appropriate in straightforward situations, such as between spouses who intend all assets to pass to each other. It can be problematic, however, in blended families or where the owner wishes to benefit children, charities, or other beneficiaries after the survivor's death.

Another consideration is the legal effect of adding a joint owner during life. Creating a joint tenancy typically requires conveying a present ownership interest to the other party. This means that the original owner is no longer the sole owner and may not be able to sell, mortgage, or otherwise encumber the property without the consent of the joint owner. In addition, the joint owner's creditors may be able to reach the property during the joint owner's lifetime, depending on state law and the form of ownership used. These risks must be weighed against the probate-avoidance benefit.

Joint ownership can also create unintended tax consequences. While probate avoidance itself does not determine tax treatment, the way property is titled can affect income tax basis adjustments at death. In many cases, property held solely by a decedent receives a full step-up in basis to fair market value at death, reducing capital gains tax if the property is later sold. Jointly owned property may receive only a partial step-up, particularly when the joint owners are not spouses. The resulting tax cost may exceed the savings from avoiding probate, especially for highly appreciated assets.

EXAMPLE

David Hernandez and his sister, Maria Hernandez, purchased a rental duplex together in California many years ago as joint tenants with right of survivorship. They chose this structure to ensure that the property would pass automatically to the survivor without probate. When David later died, Maria became the sole legal owner of the duplex with minimal administrative effort. However, the tax outcome was less favorable than expected. Because Maria already owned half of the property, only David's half received a step-up in basis to fair market value at his death. Maria's original half retained its much lower historical basis. When Maria eventually sold the property, she owed capital gains tax on the appreciation attributable to her original ownership interest. The resulting tax bill was substantial and far exceeded the legal fees that probate would have required. In hindsight, separate ownership with a full step-up at death would have produced a better overall financial result.

There is also the issue of gift tax exposure when creating joint ownership. Adding a non-spouse as a joint owner may be treated as a taxable gift of a portion of the property's value at the time of transfer. While annual exclusions and lifetime exemptions often eliminate actual tax liability, the reporting requirements and potential impact on estate planning strategies should not be ignored. What appears to be a simple change in title can have complex downstream effects.

From an estate planning perspective, joint ownership with right of survivorship works best when used selectively and in coordination with other planning tools. It is most effective for assets that the owner intends to leave outright to the surviving joint owner, without conditions or further distribution. In such cases, survivorship ownership functions as a built-in transfer mechanism that is both efficient and predictable. When more nuanced planning is required, such as staggered distributions, asset protection for beneficiaries, or tax optimization, other tools like trusts may be more appropriate.

Nevertheless, the appeal of joint ownership as a probate-avoidance device lies in its accessibility. It does not require the drafting of a will or trust, ongoing administration, or complex legal documentation. In many cases, a simple change in title or account registration is sufficient. This ease of implementation makes it particularly attractive to individuals who are reluctant to engage in formal estate planning or who have relatively simple asset structures.

In practice, many people use joint ownership incrementally, often without fully appreciating its estate planning implications. A parent may add an adult child to a bank account for convenience, intending only to facilitate bill payments. At death, however, the account passes entirely to that child by right of survivorship, regardless of what the parent's will provides. This outcome may or may not align with the parent's broader estate plan, and it can create conflict among heirs who expected a different distribution. The probate-avoidance feature works as designed, but its consequences can be misunderstood.

The automatic nature of survivorship transfers is both their strength and their limitation. Because the transfer occurs by operation of law, there is no opportunity for oversight or adjustment based on changed circumstances at death. The court does not review the fairness of the outcome or consider competing claims from other heirs. This certainty can be reassuring, but it also eliminates flexibility. Once survivorship ownership is established, it generally requires affirmative action during life to undo it.

In evaluating joint ownership with right of survivorship as a probate-avoidance strategy, it is important to distinguish between avoiding probate and avoiding estate administration entirely. While survivorship property bypasses probate, it does not necessarily avoid all post-death obligations. Estate taxes, income taxes, and creditor claims may still apply, depending on the nature of the asset and applicable law. Avoiding probate simplifies the transfer of title, but it does not eliminate the need for careful planning and compliance.

EXAMPLE

When Thomas Reynolds added his adult daughter, Emily Reynolds, to his investment account as a joint owner with right of survivorship, he believed the arrangement would eliminate all estate-related complications. When Thomas died, Emily did receive immediate ownership of the account without opening a probate case, which allowed her to access funds quickly to cover household expenses. However, the transfer did not end the estate's administrative responsibilities. Thomas's final income tax return still had to be filed, including income generated by the account before his death. In addition, the value of the account was included in determining whether estate tax filings were required, even though probate was avoided. Creditors also retained the right to assert valid claims against the estate, and Emily needed to coordinate with the estate's executor to ensure that obligations were satisfied. The survivorship feature simplified title transfer, but it did not eliminate the need for careful post-death administration and compliance.

Ultimately, joint ownership with right of survivorship is best understood as a structural solution to a procedural problem. Probate exists because ownership interests must be transferred at death. By redefining ownership so that nothing remains to be transferred, survivorship ownership sidesteps the process altogether. When used intentionally and with full awareness of its consequences, it can be an effective and elegant way to ensure that property passes quickly and privately to a surviving owner. When used casually or without coordination, it can undermine broader estate planning goals.

The enduring popularity of joint ownership reflects a common human preference for simplicity and certainty. People want to know that their spouse or partner will be able to continue living in the home, access funds, and manage assets without delay or bureaucratic hurdles. Joint ownership with right of survivorship delivers on that promise in a direct and legally robust way. Its ability to avoid probate is not a loophole or a technical trick, but a natural consequence of how ownership is defined and extinguished at death.

In the final analysis, joint ownership with right of survivorship offers a good example of how property law can shape estate outcomes without court involvement. It demonstrates that avoiding probate does not always require complex planning structures, but it also highlights the importance of understanding the legal effects of seemingly simple decisions.

Option 3: Beneficiary Designations

One of the most practical and widely used tools for avoiding probate is the beneficiary designation. Properly structured beneficiary designations allow assets to transfer directly to named individuals or entities at death, outside the probate estate, by operation of contract rather than a court order.

A beneficiary designation is a contractual instruction attached to a specific asset, directing the custodian or issuer of that asset to transfer ownership upon the death of the owner. Unlike a will, which takes effect only after probate begins, beneficiary designations operate immediately upon proof of death. The asset holder, such as a financial institution, insurance company, or retirement plan administrator, pays or transfers the asset directly to the named beneficiary once the required documentation is provided. Because the transfer is governed by contract law rather than probate law, the asset never becomes part of the probate estate and is not subject to court supervision.

Life insurance policies are one of the clearest examples of how beneficiary designations avoid probate. When a policyholder dies, the insurance company pays the death benefit directly to the named beneficiary. The proceeds do not pass through the decedent's estate unless the estate itself is named as beneficiary. As long as a living individual, trust, or qualifying entity is properly designated, the insurer has no obligation to involve the probate court. This direct transfer not only accelerates payment, often within weeks of death, but also keeps the proceeds private, since probate filings are generally public records while insurance payouts are not.

EXAMPLE

When Michael Thompson, a retired engineer in Arizona, died unexpectedly at age 68, his family faced immediate expenses. Michael had purchased a $500,000 term life insurance policy years earlier and named his daughter, Emily Thompson, as the sole beneficiary. After receiving a certified death certificate and completing a short claim form, Emily submitted the paperwork directly to the insurer. Within three weeks, the insurance company wired the proceeds to her bank account. The funds never became part of Michael's probate estate, even though his will was still being administered by the court. Creditors, the personal representative, and the probate judge had no authority over the policy proceeds. The payment remained private and was not disclosed in probate filings. Emily used the funds to pay funeral costs and retire her mortgage.

Retirement accounts function in much the same way. Accounts such as IRAs, 401(k)s, 403(b)s, and other qualified plans rely heavily on beneficiary designations. Federal law often gives beneficiary forms priority over wills, meaning that the named beneficiary receives the account regardless of what a will might say. Upon the account holder's death, the plan administrator transfers or retitles the account in the beneficiary's name or distributes funds according to plan rules. These assets bypass probate entirely unless the estate is named as beneficiary or no beneficiary designation is in place. Given that retirement accounts often represent a significant portion of an individual's wealth, beneficiary designations can remove substantial value from the probate process.

EXAMPLE

When Patricia Reynolds, a longtime school administrator in Ohio, died at age 72, her largest asset was a $900,000 403(b) account accumulated over three decades. Years earlier, Patricia had named her son, Daniel Reynolds, as the sole beneficiary on the plan's beneficiary form. Although her will directed that all assets be divided equally among her children, federal retirement plan rules controlled the account. After Patricia's death, the plan administrator requested a death certificate and beneficiary confirmation. Within a month, the account was retitled into an inherited retirement account in Daniel's name. The funds never passed through probate and were not subject to court oversight. The probate estate handled other assets, but the retirement account transferred privately outside the estate process.

Payable-on-death and transfer-on-death designations extend the same concept to non-retirement financial accounts. Many banks and brokerage firms allow account owners to name one or more beneficiaries who will receive the account balance at death. During the owner's lifetime, the beneficiary has no rights to the account and cannot access the funds. At death, the institution releases the funds directly to the beneficiary upon receipt of a death certificate and identification. The simplicity of this arrangement makes it an attractive probate-avoidance tool for checking accounts, savings accounts, certificates of deposit, and investment accounts. These designations are especially useful for individuals who want to ensure quick access to cash for survivors to cover immediate expenses.

Transfer-on-death registrations are also commonly used for securities and brokerage accounts. Rather than retitling the account during life, the owner retains full control while naming a beneficiary who will inherit the account automatically. Upon death, the brokerage firm retitles the securities in the beneficiary's name without court involvement. This mechanism avoids probate while preserving the owner's flexibility to change beneficiaries or liquidate assets during life.

Beneficiary designations are not limited to financial accounts. In many states, transfer-on-death deeds allow real estate to pass directly to a named beneficiary upon the owner's death. While the owner remains the full legal owner during life, the recorded deed specifies who will receive title at death. Because ownership transfers automatically, the property does not enter the probate estate. This can be particularly valuable for a primary residence or rental property, where probate delays could otherwise complicate occupancy, maintenance, or sale. The effectiveness of these deeds depends on state law, but where available, they represent a powerful probate-avoidance technique grounded in beneficiary designation principles.

EXAMPLE

When Laura Martinez, a widowed homeowner in Colorado, purchased her home, she later recorded a transfer-on-death deed naming her nephew, Carlos Martinez, as the beneficiary. Laura continued to live in the house, refinance the mortgage, and pay property taxes without restriction, since the deed had no effect during her lifetime. When Laura died at age 79, Carlos recorded her death certificate with the county recorder's office. Title transferred to him automatically under state law, without probate court involvement. The house never became part of Laura's probate estate, even though her will was being administered for other assets. Carlos was able to secure insurance coverage and prepare the property for sale immediately, avoiding months of delay and public court filings.

One of the key advantages of beneficiary designations is speed. Beneficiary-designated assets can often be transferred within a matter of weeks. This immediacy can be critical for surviving spouses, dependents, or other beneficiaries who rely on those assets for living expenses or debt repayment.

Privacy is also an important consideration. Transfers occur privately between the institution and the beneficiary, without public disclosure of asset values or recipient identities. For individuals concerned about confidentiality or family dynamics, this privacy can be a significant benefit.

Beneficiary designations also provide clarity and certainty. When properly completed and kept current, they leave little room for interpretation or dispute. The institution holding the asset follows the designation as written, reducing the likelihood of litigation. While beneficiary designations can be challenged in rare cases, they generally present a clear, straightforward directive.

Despite their advantages, beneficiary designations require careful coordination with the rest of an estate plan. One of the most common mistakes is failing to update designations after major life events such as marriage, divorce, birth of a child, or death of a beneficiary. Because beneficiary forms often override wills, outdated designations can lead to unintended results. For example, an ex-spouse may remain the named beneficiary on a retirement account long after a divorce, resulting in an inheritance that conflicts with the decedent's current wishes. Regular review is essential to ensure alignment with overall planning goals.

> **Tip:** A potential pitfall arises when beneficiaries are minors or individuals with special needs. Assets transferred directly through beneficiary designations typically pass outright, without the protections of a trust. For minors, this may require court-appointed guardianship, undermining the goal of avoiding probate. For beneficiaries with disabilities, an outright distribution could jeopardize their eligibility for government benefits. In such cases, naming a trust as beneficiary can preserve probate avoidance while adding necessary safeguards. The trust receives the asset directly, and the trustee manages it according to the trust's terms.

Creditor considerations also warrant attention. While beneficiary-designated assets avoid probate, they are not always immune from creditor claims. In some jurisdictions, certain creditors may have limited rights to pursue non-probate assets to satisfy outstanding debts. However, many assets such as life insurance and retirement accounts receive varying degrees of creditor protection under state or federal law. Understanding these rules is critical when using beneficiary designations as part of a broader asset protection strategy.

Tax implications must also be considered. Avoiding probate does not automatically avoid estate or income taxes. Beneficiary-designated assets are generally included in the decedent's gross estate for estate tax purposes. Additionally, beneficiaries may face income tax consequences, particularly with retirement accounts, where distributions are often taxable. Nonetheless, beneficiary designations can be coordinated with tax planning strategies, such as naming charitable beneficiaries or structuring distributions through trusts, to achieve both probate avoidance and tax efficiency.

Beneficiary designations can also be layered with other estate planning tools. Revocable living trusts, for example, are often used in conjunction with beneficiary designations. While trusts can hold many assets directly, beneficiary designations can funnel certain assets into the trust at death. This approach allows the trust to govern post-death management and distribution without requiring probate. When properly coordinated, beneficiary designations act as funding mechanisms that support the trust's objectives.

EXAMPLE

When Robert Ellis, a small business owner in California, created a revocable living trust, he transferred most of his assets into the trust during his lifetime. He also coordinated his beneficiary designations to support the trust plan. Robert named the "Robert Ellis Revocable Trust dated March 3, 2018" as beneficiary of his life insurance policy and IRA. At his death, the insurer and plan custodian paid the proceeds directly to the trust, not to Robert's probate estate. The successor trustee immediately assumed control of the funds and followed the trust terms for managing investments and making distributions to Robert's children over time. No probate court approval was required. The beneficiary designations functioned as funding tools that reinforced the trust's administration and distribution strategy.

Tip: The simplicity of beneficiary designations can be deceptive. While filling out a form may seem straightforward, the legal consequences are significant. Errors such as ambiguous language, improper beneficiary identification, or failure to name contingent beneficiaries can create confusion and delay. Naming contingent beneficiaries is especially important, as it provides a clear path if the primary beneficiary predeceases the owner. Without contingents, assets may revert to the estate and become subject to probate, defeating the original purpose.

Another consideration is equalization among heirs. Because beneficiary-designated assets pass outside the will, they can distort intended distributions if not carefully balanced. For example, one child might receive a large retirement account through a beneficiary designation, while another receives probate assets under the will. Without intentional planning, this imbalance can lead to perceived unfairness and family conflict. Estate planners often address this by adjusting beneficiary designations or using life insurance and trusts to equalize outcomes.

EXAMPLE

When Helen Foster, a retired pharmacist in New York, reviewed her estate plan, she realized that most of her wealth sat in a $1.2 million IRA naming her eldest daughter, Susan Foster, as beneficiary. Her will, however, left her remaining probate assets, worth only $300,000, to be divided equally between Susan and her younger son, Mark Foster. Without adjustment, Susan would receive far more than Mark. Working with an estate planner, Helen changed the IRA beneficiary to a trust that split distributions evenly and purchased a modest life insurance policy naming Mark as beneficiary. When Helen later died, the coordinated plan produced roughly equal outcomes. The adjustments prevented resentment and reduced the risk of post-death disputes between siblings.

In practice, beneficiary designations are most effective when viewed as part of an integrated estate plan rather than standalone solutions. They work best when coordinated with wills, trusts, powers of attorney, and overall financial objectives. Regular reviews, especially after major life changes, help ensure that designations continue to reflect current intentions and legal requirements.

In summary, beneficiary designations are a powerful and flexible tool for avoiding probate. By allowing assets to transfer directly to named beneficiaries through contractual arrangements, they bypass court supervision, reduce costs, accelerate distributions, and preserve privacy. They are particularly effective for life insurance, retirement accounts, financial accounts, and in some cases real estate. However, their effectiveness depends on careful drafting, regular updates, and coordination with the broader estate plan. When used thoughtfully, beneficiary designations can significantly streamline the transfer of wealth and reduce the administrative burden on survivors, fulfilling one of the central goals of modern estate planning.

Option 4: Payable-on-Death Accounts

Payable on death accounts are a widely used estate planning mechanism that allow individuals to transfer certain financial assets directly to named beneficiaries at death without the need for probate. Their appeal lies in their simplicity, low cost, and effectiveness in bypassing what can otherwise be a time-consuming and public court process. Understanding how payable on death accounts function, why they avoid probate, and how they fit into a broader estate plan requires an appreciation of both their legal structure and their practical consequences.

At its core, a payable on death account is a contractual arrangement between an account holder and a financial institution. The account is owned entirely by the depositor during life. The beneficiary designation has no legal effect while the depositor is alive and retains full control over the account. The depositor can withdraw funds, change beneficiaries, or close the account at any time. The beneficiary has no ownership interest, no right to information, and no ability to interfere with the account during the depositor's lifetime. This feature distinguishes payable on death accounts from joint accounts, which often convey present ownership interests that can create unintended tax or control consequences.

Financial institutions are authorized by state statutes to recognize payable on death designations. Once the institution receives satisfactory proof of death, typically a death certificate and beneficiary identification, it releases the funds directly to the named beneficiary. The institution does not wait for probate court approval and does not require letters testamentary[2] or letters of administration[3]. This direct transfer is the essence of probate avoidance. The asset never becomes part of the probate estate because legal title shifts immediately upon death pursuant to the account agreement.

This immediacy can be especially valuable. Probate often takes months and, in some jurisdictions, more than a year to complete. During that time, assets may be frozen or inaccessible, which can create liquidity problems for surviving family members. Payable on death accounts provide near-immediate access to funds for beneficiaries, allowing them to cover funeral costs, living expenses, or other immediate financial needs without delay. From a practical standpoint, this is one of the most compelling reasons why individuals use these accounts.

Another reason payable on death accounts avoid probate is that they are governed primarily by contract law rather than succession law. The beneficiary designation is treated as a binding contractual instruction to the financial institution. Courts generally uphold these designations even if they conflict with the provisions of a will. For example, a will might state that all assets should be divided equally among children, but if a payable on death account names only one child as beneficiary, the financial institution will pay the entire account balance to that child. The account does not pass

[2] Letters testamentary are court-issued documents that formally authorize an executor named in a will to administer the decedent's estate, including collecting assets, paying debts, and distributing property according to the will.

[3] Letters of administration are court-issued documents that authorize a person to manage and distribute a deceased individual's estate when the person died without a will or did not name an executor.

under the will because it is not part of the probate estate. This characteristic underscores both the power and the risk of payable on death designations. They must be coordinated carefully with the rest of the estate plan to avoid unintended distributions.

From a legal perspective, payable on death accounts are sometimes described as non-probate transfers or will substitutes. They function similarly to other beneficiary-designated assets such as life insurance policies and retirement accounts. The common thread is that ownership transfers automatically at death based on a beneficiary designation. Because probate courts have jurisdiction primarily over probate assets, they generally have no authority over payable on death accounts. This separation is what allows the accounts to bypass court supervision.

The simplicity of establishing a payable on death account further enhances its appeal. Most banks and brokerage firms offer standard beneficiary designation forms. Completing the designation typically requires only basic information such as the beneficiary's name and relationship. There is no need for notarization, witnesses, or legal drafting. In contrast, creating and maintaining a trust, another common probate-avoidance tool, often involves legal fees, ongoing administration, and more complex documentation. For individuals with relatively straightforward estates, payable on death accounts can achieve many of the same probate-avoidance benefits at a fraction of the cost.

Note: The effectiveness of payable on death accounts in avoiding probate depends on proper implementation. The account must be titled correctly and the beneficiary designation must be valid under state law. If no beneficiary is named, or if all named beneficiaries predecease the account holder and no contingent beneficiaries are listed, the account typically reverts to the decedent's estate and becomes subject to probate. Similarly, ambiguous or improperly completed designations can lead to disputes that may draw the account into litigation, undermining the very goal of probate avoidance.

Another important consideration is creditor claims. While payable on death accounts avoid probate, they do not necessarily avoid the decedent's creditors. State laws vary, but in many jurisdictions, creditors may be able to pursue non-probate assets if the probate estate is insufficient to satisfy debts. This means that while the account bypasses the probate process, it is not entirely immune from post-death claims. Nonetheless, the procedural advantages remain significant because the transfer to the beneficiary is not delayed by routine probate administration.

EXAMPLE

When Robert Ellis died unexpectedly, his primary bank account passed directly to his daughter under a payable on death designation. She was able to access the funds within weeks, avoiding the delays of probate and using the money to cover immediate expenses. However, Robert had outstanding medical bills and credit card debt that exceeded the value of his remaining probate assets. Because the probate estate was insufficient, creditors asserted claims against the non-probate account under state law. Although the funds had already transferred to the daughter, she was required to work with the estate's administrator to resolve valid claims. Even so, the payable on death structure spared the account from months of court supervision, preserving much of its administrative efficiency.

Payable on death accounts also offer privacy advantages. Probate is a public process. Wills, inventories, and accountings filed with the court are generally accessible to the public. Payable on death transfers occur outside this system. The amount in the account and the identity of the beneficiary are typically known only to the financial institution and the parties involved. For individuals concerned about confidentiality, this privacy can be a meaningful benefit.

The flexibility of payable on death accounts further enhances their utility. Beneficiaries can usually be changed at any time without tax consequences or legal formalities. This allows the account holder to respond easily to life changes such as marriage, divorce, births, deaths, or shifts in personal relationships. From an estate planning standpoint, this flexibility reduces the risk that outdated documents will control asset distribution. However, it also increases the importance of periodic review. An old beneficiary designation that no longer reflects the account holder's intent will still control the transfer, regardless of what a will or trust might say.

In blended families and second marriages, payable on death accounts are often used strategically to direct specific assets to particular individuals. For example, a person might leave a residence to a surviving spouse through a will but designate adult children from a prior marriage as beneficiaries of certain financial accounts. Because the payable on death account bypasses probate, it ensures that the designated beneficiary receives the asset directly, without being subject to potential disputes during estate administration. While this can be effective, it also raises fairness and transparency issues that should be addressed through careful planning and communication.

Tax considerations also play a role, though they do not affect probate avoidance directly. For income tax purposes, beneficiaries generally receive a step-up in basis for assets held in payable on death accounts, just as they would for probate assets. For estate tax purposes, the value of the account is typically included in the decedent's gross estate. Thus, payable on death accounts avoid probate but not estate taxation. This distinction is important because some individuals mistakenly believe that avoiding probate also avoids taxes. In reality, probate is a procedural issue, while taxation is governed by separate rules.

EXAMPLE

When Linda Parker named her son as the beneficiary of her payable on death brokerage account, she believed the designation would simplify matters after her death. Upon Linda's passing, the account transferred quickly to her son without probate, allowing him immediate control of the investments. At tax time, however, he learned that the account's fair market value at Linda's date of death was included in her taxable estate. While he benefited from a step-up in basis, eliminating capital gains on prior appreciation, the estate still had to consider federal estate tax exposure.

The relationship between payable on death accounts and trusts is another area where probate avoidance is relevant. Some individuals name a trust as the beneficiary of a payable on death account. This approach can combine the simplicity of a payable on death designation with the control and protections of a trust. The account still avoids probate because it passes directly to the trust, and the trust terms then govern how the funds are managed and distributed. This can be especially useful when beneficiaries are minors, have special needs, or require structured distributions over time.

Despite their advantages, payable on death accounts are not a universal solution. They are best suited for financial accounts such as bank deposits, certificates of deposit, and brokerage accounts. They are not applicable to all asset types. Real estate, for example, requires different mechanisms to avoid probate, such as transfer on death deeds or trust ownership, depending on state law. An estate plan that relies solely on payable on death accounts may leave other assets exposed to probate unless additional planning steps are taken.

There is also the risk of inconsistency. Because payable on death designations operate independently of wills, it is possible for an individual's overall distribution plan to become fragmented. One beneficiary might receive a substantial account directly, while others receive less through probate, even if the intent was equal distribution. Without careful coordination, payable on death accounts can undermine the coherence of an estate plan. This is not a flaw in the mechanism itself but a reminder that probate avoidance tools must be used deliberately.

In practice, many individuals use payable on death accounts as a foundational element of a broader probate-avoidance strategy. By designating beneficiaries on most financial accounts, they can significantly reduce the size of the probate estate. The remaining assets may be minimal, making probate simpler, faster, and less expensive. In some cases, probate may be avoided entirely if all significant assets transfer through non-probate mechanisms. This outcome is particularly attractive in states where probate is costly or burdensome.

In Which States is Probate Unusually Expensive?

Probate costs vary widely by state, but probate is often considered unusually expensive in states where statutes permit percentage-based fees, require extensive court supervision, or impose mandatory attorney involvement. The states most often cited include:

- *California*. Statutory attorney and executor fees are based on a percentage of the gross estate value, not the complexity of the work, which can make probate very costly for real estate–heavy estates.
- *Florida*. Attorney representation is effectively mandatory, and probate can be lengthy and expensive, especially for formal administration.
- *New York*. Court procedures are detailed and time-consuming, and legal fees are often high due to complexity and required filings.
- *New Jersey*. Executor commissions and attorney fees can be substantial, particularly for larger estates.
- *Illinois*. Formal probate involves significant court oversight, which increases administrative and legal costs.

Another subtle benefit of payable on death accounts is administrative efficiency. Financial institutions are accustomed to processing beneficiary claims and have standardized procedures in place. This reduces the likelihood of administrative errors and delays. In contrast, probate administration can be affected by court backlogs, procedural complexities, and disputes among heirs. By shifting asset transfers into a more streamlined system, payable on death accounts reduce friction at a time when beneficiaries are often dealing with emotional and logistical challenges.

From a policy perspective, legislatures have encouraged the use of payable on death accounts as a way to simplify wealth transfer for ordinary individuals. Statutory frameworks governing these accounts are designed to provide clarity and predictability. Courts generally interpret beneficiary designations strictly, favoring the expressed intent on the account form. This legal certainty reinforces the probate-avoidance function by minimizing ambiguity about who is entitled to the asset.

In conclusion, payable on death accounts avoid probate because they transfer ownership by contract rather than by will, allowing assets to pass directly to named beneficiaries upon death. They offer speed, privacy, simplicity, and flexibility, making them an effective tool for many estate plans. However, their effectiveness depends on proper designation, regular review, and coordination with other planning documents. When used thoughtfully, payable on death accounts can significantly reduce or even eliminate the need for probate, easing the administrative burden on survivors while ensuring that assets pass according to the account holder's intent.

Option 5: Transfer-on-Death Registration

Transfer on death registration is a legal mechanism designed to simplify the passage of property at death while avoiding the cost, delay, and publicity of probate. At its core, it allows an owner to designate a beneficiary who will automatically receive the asset upon the owner's death, without the asset becoming part of the probate estate. This concept rests on a simple idea: ownership does not actually change during the owner's lifetime, but the law recognizes a prearranged instruction that takes effect only at death. Because the transfer is automatic and occurs by operation of law, the probate court is bypassed entirely for that asset.

The most familiar example of transfer on death principles appears in financial accounts. Bank accounts, brokerage accounts, and retirement accounts frequently allow beneficiaries to be designated using pay-on-death or transfer-on-death forms. In these cases, the account owner retains full control during life. The beneficiary has no ownership rights, cannot access the account, and cannot interfere with the owner's decisions. The owner can change or revoke the designation at any time, so long as they have legal capacity. At death, however, the financial institution transfers ownership directly to the named beneficiary upon presentation of a death certificate and required identification. The court is not involved, and the executor has no authority over the account.

EXAMPLE

Margaret Lewis maintained a brokerage account she had built over decades of careful investing. While alive, she alone made all investment decisions, traded securities, and withdrew funds as needed. Years earlier, she completed a transfer-on-death form naming her niece, Claire, as beneficiary. Claire had no access to the account and could not view balances or influence Margaret's choices. Margaret later changed the beneficiary once, then changed it back, demonstrating her continued control. When Margaret died, Claire presented a death certificate and identification to the brokerage firm. Within days, the account was retitled in Claire's name. No probate court approval was required, and the executor of Margaret's estate had no authority over the account.

The same concept has been extended to other types of property through statute. Many states allow transfer on death registration for securities under the Uniform Transfer on Death Securities Registration Act. Under this framework, stocks, bonds, mutual funds, and similar instruments can be registered via a transfer on death form. The registration itself states that ownership passes to the named beneficiary upon death. Until then, the owner remains the sole owner and can sell, gift, or re-register the securities without the beneficiary's consent. This statutory clarity is what keeps the asset out of probate, because the title mechanism itself defines the post-death transfer.

What is the Uniform Transfer on Death Securities Registration Act?

The Uniform Transfer on Death Securities Registration Act is a uniform state law that allows securities to be registered in transfer-on-death form, naming a beneficiary to receive the asset at the owner's death. During the owner's lifetime, the beneficiary has no ownership rights, and the owner retains full control, including the ability to sell, transfer, or change the designation. At death, the securities pass directly to the named beneficiary outside of probate, subject to applicable creditor and tax rules.

Real estate is another area where transfer on death registration has gained traction. Traditionally, avoiding probate for real property required more complex planning tools such as revocable living trusts or joint ownership arrangements. In response, many states adopted transfer on death deeds, sometimes called beneficiary deeds. These deeds are recorded during the owner's lifetime and name a beneficiary who will receive the property at death. The deed does not give the beneficiary any present interest. The owner can sell the property, mortgage it, or revoke the deed without the beneficiary's permission. At death, title transfers automatically to the beneficiary, typically through an affidavit process[4] rather than a court proceeding.

The probate avoidance benefit of transfer on death registration arises from how ownership is defined at the moment of death. Probate only applies to property that is owned by the decedent individually at death and does not have an alternative transfer

---

[4] An affidavit process is a simplified legal procedure in which a sworn written statement is used to establish facts or transfer certain assets without formal court involvement.

mechanism. Assets that pass by contract or by statute, such as life insurance, retirement accounts, jointly owned property with rights of survivorship, and transfer on death assets, fall outside the probate estate. Transfer on death registration effectively converts individually owned property into property with a built-in nonprobate transfer instruction. Because the transfer is already defined and legally enforceable, the probate court has nothing to administer.

Another advantage of transfer on death registration is privacy. These transfers occur privately between the institution or recorder's office and the beneficiary. There is no public accounting of the asset value, no disclosure of beneficiary identities in court filings, and no centralized record that can be easily searched. For individuals concerned about confidentiality, this is a meaningful benefit.

Speed is also a significant factor. A transfer on death asset can often be distributed within weeks of death. A beneficiary can present a death certificate, complete standard forms, and receive control of the asset quickly. This can be especially important when beneficiaries rely on the asset for immediate financial support or when liquidity is needed to cover funeral costs or ongoing expenses.

Transfer on death registration also offers flexibility during life. Because the beneficiary designation does not create a present interest, the owner is free to change beneficiaries as circumstances evolve. Marriages, divorces, births, deaths, and changes in relationships can all be accommodated with a relatively simple administrative update. This stands in contrast to some probate avoidance strategies that require retitling assets or creating irrevocable interests that are difficult to unwind. In that sense, transfer on death registration combines simplicity with control.

Despite its benefits, transfer on death registration is not a complete substitute for comprehensive estate planning. It avoids probate only for the specific assets that are properly registered. Any assets that lack a transfer on death designation and are owned solely by the decedent will still pass through probate. As a result, incomplete implementation can undermine the intended efficiency. For example, an individual may register a brokerage account as transfer on death but forget to address a checking account or a piece of real estate in a state that does not recognize transfer on death deeds. Those assets will still require probate administration.

Another limitation involves creditor rights. While transfer on death assets bypass probate, they are not necessarily immune from claims by creditors of the decedent. Many state statutes provide that beneficiaries who receive assets by transfer on death remain liable to the extent of the asset value for enforceable debts, taxes, and expenses of administration if the probate estate is insufficient. This means that transfer on death registration avoids the probate process but does not eliminate legitimate obligations. Creditors may still pursue recovery through alternative legal means.

Tax considerations also require careful attention. Transfer on death registration does not avoid estate tax or inheritance tax where applicable. The asset is still included in the decedent's gross estate for federal estate tax purposes. However, in many cases, beneficiaries receive a step-up in basis equal to the asset's fair market value at death, which can be a significant income tax advantage if the asset is later sold. This tax treatment is similar to that of assets passing through probate or through a revocable trust, so transfer on death registration generally does not create adverse tax consequences by itself.

There are also practical risks associated with beneficiary designations. If a beneficiary predeceases the owner and no contingent beneficiary is named, the transfer on death designation may fail, causing the asset to revert to the probate estate. Similarly, vague or outdated designations can create confusion or disputes. For example, naming "my children" without clarification can lead to disagreements if family circumstances are complex. Careful drafting and periodic review are essential to ensure that the transfer on death registration operates as intended.

Another consideration is coordination with the overall estate plan. Transfer on death designations override provisions in a will. If a will directs that all assets be divided equally among heirs, but a major asset is registered to transfer on death to a single individual, the will does not control that asset. This can unintentionally skew distributions and create perceived unfairness among beneficiaries. Effective use of transfer on death registration requires alignment with testamentary documents to avoid conflicting instructions.

In family situations involving minor beneficiaries or beneficiaries with special needs, transfer on death registration may be inappropriate unless paired with additional planning. Assets transferred directly to a minor may require the appointment of a guardian, undermining the goal of simplicity. Similarly, direct transfers to individuals receiving needs-based public benefits can jeopardize eligibility. In such cases, trusts are often a more suitable vehicle, even though they may involve greater upfront complexity.

EXAMPLE

Thomas Reed named his two children as transfer on death beneficiaries on his brokerage account, assuming the arrangement would simplify matters. When he died unexpectedly, one child was seventeen and the other was an adult receiving Supplemental Security Income due to a disability. The financial institution could not release funds to the minor without a court-appointed guardian, forcing the family into probate court despite Thomas's intentions. Meanwhile, the adult child's direct inheritance temporarily disqualified her from public benefits until the funds were spent down. Had Thomas instead directed the account into a properly drafted trust, a trustee could have managed distributions for the minor until adulthood and preserved benefit eligibility through a special needs trust. The trust would have added planning complexity, but it would have avoided court involvement and unintended harm to both children.

From an administrative standpoint, transfer on death registration reduces the burden on executors. Because the asset does not pass through probate, the executor does not need to inventory it, manage it, or distribute it. This can reduce executor liability and streamline the administration of any remaining probate assets. For modest estates, the cumulative effect can be significant, potentially eliminating the need for formal probate altogether if most assets are properly designated.

The effectiveness of transfer on death registration ultimately depends on statutory recognition and proper execution. Each state defines the scope, formalities, and limitations of transfer on death mechanisms. Some states allow its broad use for real estate and securities, while others restrict or prohibit certain applications. Failure to comply with statutory requirements, such as proper recording of a transfer on death deed or correct account registration language, can invalidate the designation. As a result, professional guidance is often advisable when implementing these tools, especially for high-value or complex assets.

In practice, transfer on death registration is best viewed as a surgical tool rather than a universal solution. It excels at addressing specific assets where probate avoidance provides the greatest benefit, such as financial accounts or single-owner real estate. It is particularly attractive for individuals with relatively straightforward estates who want to minimize administrative friction without establishing trusts. When combined thoughtfully with a will or trust, it can form part of a cohesive strategy that balances efficiency, control, and clarity.

In narrative terms, the appeal of transfer on death registration lies in its alignment with how people intuitively think about ownership and legacy. The owner retains control during life, names who should receive the asset at death, and relies on a legal mechanism that makes the transfer automatic and predictable. The probate court, with its formalities and delays, is removed from the equation for that asset. The result is a quieter, faster, and more direct transition of property that reflects the owner's intent with minimal friction.

Option 6: Transfer-on-Death Deeds for Real Estate

Transfer on death deeds for real estate are a statutory mechanism that allow an owner to designate one or more beneficiaries who will automatically receive title to the property upon the owner's death, without the need for probate. At their core, these deeds are designed to reconcile two competing objectives that frequently arise in estate planning: retaining full ownership and control of real estate during life, while ensuring a smooth and inexpensive transfer of that property at death. By postponing the transfer of ownership until death and avoiding the creation of a present property interest in the beneficiary, a transfer on death deed can bypass probate while preserving flexibility for the owner.

For real estate, probate often involves filing a petition with the court, obtaining authority to act on behalf of the estate, providing notice to interested parties and creditors, and eventually receiving court approval to transfer title. This process can be time-consuming, public, and costly. Legal fees, appraisal costs, court costs, and delays are common, and in some jurisdictions probate proceedings can extend for a year or more. A transfer on death deed is intended to eliminate the need for that process for the covered real estate by allowing title to pass by operation of law at death.

The defining feature of a transfer on death deed is that it has no legal effect during the owner's lifetime beyond expressing an intent. The owner retains complete ownership, including the right to sell the property, mortgage it, lease it, or revoke or change the deed at any time. Because no present interest is conveyed to the beneficiary, the beneficiary has no legal rights in the property while the owner is alive. This distinction is critical, because it differentiates a transfer on death deed from other probate-avoidance techniques such as joint tenancy with right of survivorship or lifetime gifts. In joint tenancy, the co-owner acquires an immediate ownership interest, which can expose the property to that person's creditors, marital disputes, or unintended tax consequences. With a transfer on death deed, none of those risks arise during the owner's lifetime.

EXAMPLE

Maria Alvarez owned a small rental house in Arizona and wanted it to pass to her niece, Elena, without probate. She recorded a transfer on death deed, naming Elena as beneficiary. During Maria's lifetime, nothing changed. Maria continued to collect rent, refinanced the mortgage, and later leased the property to new tenants without Elena's consent. Elena had no right to enter the property, no claim to rental income, and no exposure to liability if a tenant was injured. When Maria briefly considered selling the house, she knew she could revoke the deed at any time. By contrast, had Maria added Elena as a joint tenant, Elena's personal creditors or divorce could have threatened the property. Only at Maria's death did ownership transfer automatically to Elena.

When the owner dies, the transfer on death deed becomes operative. The beneficiary typically records a death certificate and, in some jurisdictions, an affidavit or declaration confirming the owner's death and the beneficiary's entitlement. Once these documents are recorded in the land records, title passes to the beneficiary without court involvement. There is no requirement for a probate judge to approve the transfer, no executor or personal representative needs authority to sign a deed, and no probate estate must be opened solely for that property. From a practical standpoint, this means the beneficiary can take control of the property more quickly and with significantly lower transaction costs.

The simplicity of this mechanism is one of its principal advantages. A transfer on death deed is usually a short, standardized document authorized by statute. Execution requirements are generally similar to those for other deeds, such as being in writing, signed by the owner, and properly notarized. Most states require the deed to be recorded in the public land records before the owner's death for it to be effective. If the deed is not recorded during the owner's lifetime, it is typically void, and the property will instead pass through probate or under other applicable title arrangements. This requirement reinforces the importance of completing the planning process fully rather than leaving it as an informal or unfinished intention.

From an estate planning perspective, the ability to avoid probate is often closely linked to privacy. A transfer on death deed operates outside the probate court, and although the deed itself is recorded and therefore public, it does not require the same level of disclosure about the rest of the estate. For individuals who value discretion or wish to limit public exposure of their affairs, this can be a meaningful benefit.

Transfer on death deeds also offer flexibility in beneficiary designations. An owner can name one or multiple beneficiaries, and many statutes permit the designation of alternate beneficiaries in case the primary beneficiary predeceases the owner. This feature allows for straightforward contingency planning without the need for a more complex trust structure. If circumstances change, such as a change in family relationships or estate planning goals, the owner can revoke the existing deed and record a new one. Revocation is typically accomplished by recording a formal revocation document or by recording a subsequent transfer on death deed that expressly supersedes the prior one.

The use of transfer on death deeds can be particularly effective for individuals whose primary asset is their home or a small number of real estate holdings. In these cases, opening a full probate estate may feel disproportionate to the size or complexity of the assets involved. A properly executed transfer on death deed allows that property to move directly to the intended recipient with minimal administrative burden. This can be especially important for surviving family members who may rely on immediate access to the property for housing or income.

Another important aspect of probate avoidance through transfer on death deeds is the treatment of creditor claims. Although the property passes outside of probate, it is not necessarily insulated from the decedent's creditors. Many statutes provide that the beneficiary takes the property subject to existing liens, mortgages, and encumbrances. In addition, some states allow estate creditors to pursue claims against the transferred property for a limited period after death, particularly if the probate estate is insufficient to satisfy valid debts. This means that while probate is avoided procedurally, the substantive rights of creditors are often preserved. From a planning standpoint, this balances efficiency with fairness and reduces the risk that transfer on death deeds could be used to evade legitimate obligations.

EXAMPLE

Daniel Chen owned a modest home and recorded a transfer on death deed naming his son, Eric, as beneficiary. At Daniel's death, the house transferred directly to Eric without probate. However, the property still carried a mortgage and a recorded home equity lien, both of which Eric became responsible for after the transfer. In addition, Daniel had significant medical bills at death, and his probate estate contained little cash. Under state law, the hospital was permitted to pursue its claim against the transferred property within a limited statutory period. Eric could not simply ignore the debt because the house passed outside probate. The deed avoided court administration and delay, but it did not eliminate Daniel's legitimate obligations.

Tax considerations also play a role in evaluating transfer on death deeds as a probate-avoidance tool. Because no transfer occurs during the owner's lifetime, there is generally no gift tax consequence when the deed is executed or recorded. At death, the beneficiary typically receives a stepped-up basis in the property equal to its fair market value at the date of death, assuming current federal tax law applies. This is a significant advantage compared to lifetime gifts, which carry over the donor's basis and can result in larger capital gains when the property is eventually sold. From an income tax perspective, transfer on death deeds often achieve a favorable outcome while still avoiding probate.

Transfer on death deeds also integrate relatively easily with other estate planning documents. An owner can still have a will that disposes of other assets, and the existence of a transfer on death deed does not generally conflict with the will as long as the documents are consistent. In most jurisdictions, the deed controls the disposition of the specific real estate it covers, regardless of what the will says. This underscores the importance of coordination. If a will purports to leave the property to one person but a transfer on death deed names a different beneficiary, the deed will usually prevail. Proper planning requires careful review to ensure that all documents reflect the same intentions.

Despite their advantages, transfer on death deeds are not a universal solution, and understanding their limitations is part of using them effectively to avoid probate. They are typically authorized only for real estate, not for personal property or financial accounts. They also do not provide the management features of a trust, such as the ability to control how property is used or distributed over time. Once the owner dies, the beneficiary receives the property outright, subject only to existing legal constraints. For owners who wish to impose conditions, stagger distributions, or provide long-term oversight, a trust may be more appropriate even though it involves greater complexity.

Family dynamics can also influence the suitability of a transfer on death deed. Because the transfer occurs automatically at death, there is little opportunity for mediation or adjustment if disputes arise among heirs. While probate itself can be contentious, it does provide a formal forum for resolving disputes under court supervision. A transfer on death deed bypasses that forum, which can be an advantage in uncomplicated situations but a drawback in families with a history of conflict. In such cases, clear communication and comprehensive planning become even more important.

Note: The effectiveness of a transfer on death deed in avoiding probate depends on strict compliance with statutory requirements. Courts generally interpret these statutes narrowly, and mistakes in execution or recording can render the deed invalid. Common errors include failing to record the deed before death, improperly identifying the property or beneficiary, or failing to meet notarization or witness requirements. When a deed is invalid, the property will typically fall back into the probate estate, defeating the original purpose. As a result, professional guidance is often advisable, even though the concept itself is relatively straightforward.

In multi-state situations, additional care is required. Real estate is governed by the law of the state in which it is located, not the state of the owner's residence. A transfer on death deed that is valid in one state may not be recognized in another if that state has not adopted enabling legislation or has different requirements. For owners with property in multiple states, transfer on death deeds can still be used strategically, but each property must be evaluated under the applicable local law. When used correctly, they can reduce or eliminate the need for ancillary probate proceedings in multiple jurisdictions.

From a broader policy perspective, transfer on death deeds reflect a legislative effort to simplify wealth transfer for ordinary property owners. They offer a middle ground between informal arrangements that may fail legally and more sophisticated structures like trusts that may be unnecessary for smaller estates. By allowing owners to retain control during life and transfer property efficiently at death, these deeds align legal formality with practical needs. Their growing adoption across states suggests a recognition that probate avoidance, when done transparently and with safeguards for creditors and heirs, serves the public interest.

In practical terms, the use of a transfer on death deed often brings peace of mind. Owners know that their real estate will pass directly to the intended beneficiary without delay or court involvement. Beneficiaries, in turn, are spared the administrative and emotional burden of probate at a time when they may already be dealing with loss. While no estate planning tool is entirely risk-free, transfer on death deeds offer a relatively simple, flexible, and cost-effective way to avoid probate for real estate, provided they are used thoughtfully and in compliance with applicable law.

Option 7: Lifetime Gifts

One of the most effective and widely used strategies for avoiding probate is the use of lifetime gifts. By transferring the ownership of assets during life rather than at death, an individual can reduce the size of the probate estate, streamline the transfer of wealth, and achieve broader personal, tax, and family objectives.

At its core, probate applies only to assets that are owned by the decedent at death and that do not pass automatically by operation of law or contract. Property that is no longer owned at death, because it was previously gifted away, falls outside the probate system entirely. Lifetime gifts therefore function by changing the timing of ownership transfer. Instead of assets moving from the decedent to heirs through a will and probate court, ownership changes while the donor is alive, leaving nothing for the court to administer with respect to those assets. When used intentionally and consistently, this approach can dramatically simplify estate settlement.

Lifetime gifts can take many forms, ranging from simple cash transfers to sophisticated conveyances of business interests or real estate. A straightforward example is the annual gifting of cash to children or other family members. Once the cash is transferred and control is relinquished, the donor no longer owns the asset. If the donor later dies, that cash is not part of the probate estate because it is already owned by the recipient. Over time, repeated lifetime gifts can significantly reduce the value of assets that would otherwise be subject to probate administration.

The probate-avoidance benefit becomes more pronounced when lifetime gifts are used for high-value or administratively complex assets. Real estate is a common example. Real property owned solely in an individual's name typically requires probate to clear title after death. By transferring ownership during life, either outright or through a trust structure, the donor removes the property from the probate estate. If done correctly, the recipient already holds legal title at death, and no court involvement is required to effectuate the transfer. This can be especially valuable when property is located in multiple states, since probate would otherwise be required in each jurisdiction.

Closely held business interests also lend themselves to lifetime gifting strategies. Shares of a family business, partnership interests, or membership units in a limited liability company can be gifted gradually over time. As ownership shifts to the next generation, the portion remaining in the donor's estate shrinks. At death, probate may still be required for residual assets, but the business itself may already be largely or entirely outside the estate. This not only avoids probate for the business interests but can also ease succession by allowing the donor to observe and guide the transition while alive.

The use of lifetime gifts to avoid probate is closely intertwined with broader estate planning objectives, including privacy. Lifetime gifts are private transactions. Once assets are transferred during life, there is no public accounting of those transfers in probate court. For individuals concerned about confidentiality, especially those with substantial wealth or complex family relationships, lifetime gifting offers a way to transfer assets quietly and efficiently.

Another advantage of lifetime gifts is administrative simplicity for heirs. Lifetime gifts, by definition, place assets in the hands of recipients immediately or upon the terms established at the time of the gift. When death occurs, there is less delay, fewer legal fees, and less uncertainty. The estate administration process becomes simpler because there are fewer assets to marshal, value, and distribute.

That said, effective use of lifetime gifts requires careful consideration of control. Once a gift is completed, the donor generally cannot reclaim the asset. This loss of control is both the defining feature and the primary risk of lifetime gifting. For probate avoidance to be successful, the donor must genuinely transfer ownership rather than merely attempting to disguise continued control. Courts and tax authorities scrutinize arrangements where the donor retains excessive rights or benefits, which can undermine both probate and tax objectives.

EXAMPLE

Thomas Reed wanted to avoid probate by giving his vacation cabin to his daughter, Lauren, during his lifetime. He signed a deed transferring title to her, believing the matter was settled. However, Thomas continued to use the cabin exclusively, paid all expenses, rented it out in his own name, and told others it was still his property. When Thomas later faced creditor issues and died unexpectedly, the transfer was challenged. The court concluded that Thomas had never truly relinquished control and treated the cabin as part of his estate. The attempted gift failed to achieve probate avoidance and created tax uncertainty. Had Thomas been prepared to surrender ownership and allow Lauren to exercise genuine control, the gift could have been effective. Instead, retaining benefits undermined the planning objective.

To address control concerns, many lifetime gifting strategies involve partial or conditional transfers. For example, a donor may gift a remainder interest in property while retaining a life estate. The donor continues to live in or use the property during life, but legal ownership of the remainder passes to the recipient. At death, the life estate terminates automatically, and full ownership vests in the recipient without probate. While such arrangements must be structured carefully to comply with applicable law, they illustrate how lifetime gifts can balance probate avoidance with practical living needs.

EXAMPLE

Eleanor Whitman owned her primary residence and wanted it to pass to her nephew, James, without probate, but she was not willing to give up the right to live there. On her attorney's advice, Eleanor deeded the house to James while reserving a life estate for herself. Eleanor continued to occupy the home, paid property taxes, and maintained insurance, just as before. James held a vested remainder interest but had no right to possess or sell the property during Eleanor's lifetime. When Eleanor later moved to assisted living and then passed away, her life estate ended automatically. Full ownership transferred to James by operation of law, with no probate court involvement. The arrangement preserved Eleanor's control during life while ensuring a smooth, probate-free transfer at death.

Trusts are another powerful vehicle for lifetime gifting and probate avoidance. When assets are transferred into an irrevocable trust during life, ownership shifts from the individual to the trust. Because the trust, not the individual, owns the assets, they are not part of the probate estate. The trust instrument governs how assets are managed and distributed, both during the donor's life and after death. This approach allows the donor to set terms and protections for beneficiaries while still achieving probate avoidance.

Even simpler trust arrangements can serve probate avoidance goals. By gifting assets into a trust for the benefit of children or grandchildren, the donor ensures that those assets pass according to the trust's terms without court involvement. Unlike wills, which only become operative at death and must pass through probate, trusts operate continuously. Assets transferred during life never enter the probate system because they are not owned by the decedent at death.

The relationship between lifetime gifts and tax considerations often influences probate planning, though the two concepts are distinct. Probate avoidance focuses on the method of transfer, while tax planning focuses on the cost of transfer. In many cases, lifetime gifts serve both purposes simultaneously. By reducing the size of the estate, lifetime gifts can lower estate tax exposure while also shrinking the probate estate. However, even individuals who are not subject to estate tax may find probate avoidance compelling on its own due to administrative and personal considerations.

Note: Timing plays a critical role in the effectiveness of lifetime gifting as a probate avoidance strategy. Gifts made early allow more assets to be removed from the estate and provide greater certainty that the transfers will be respected. Last-minute gifts made shortly before death may raise questions about capacity, undue influence, or incomplete transfer, potentially leading to disputes or litigation.

Family dynamics are another important factor. Lifetime gifts allow donors to observe how recipients manage assets and to adjust future gifting accordingly. This can be particularly valuable when the goal is not only probate avoidance but also preparing heirs for financial responsibility. By transferring assets gradually, donors can provide guidance and oversight that would not be possible if all transfers occurred at death through probate.

However, lifetime gifts are not without drawbacks. From a probate perspective, improper or uneven gifting can actually increase conflict if heirs perceive favoritism or lack transparency. Because lifetime gifts bypass the formal structure of probate, there is no court-mandated accounting unless one is voluntarily provided. This makes communication and documentation essential. Clear records of gifts and the intent behind them can prevent misunderstandings and disputes after death.

EXAMPLE

Margaret Lewis had three children and began making substantial lifetime gifts to her youngest son, Daniel, to help him start a business. She did not document the transfers or explain her intentions to the other children. When Margaret later died, most of her remaining assets passed through probate and were divided equally. Daniel's siblings were surprised to learn that he had already received significant support and believed the outcome was unfair. Because the gifts occurred outside probate, there was no formal accounting to explain them, and resentment escalated into litigation. Had Margaret clearly documented the gifts and stated whether they were intended as advances on inheritance or separate assistance, much of the conflict could have been avoided. The lack of transparency, rather than the gifts themselves, created the dispute.

Another consideration is liquidity. By gifting away assets, a donor reduces the pool of resources available for personal needs, emergencies, or long-term care. While probate avoidance is a legitimate objective, it should not come at the expense of financial security during life. Effective planning balances the desire to transfer assets early with the need to retain sufficient resources. In many cases, donors combine lifetime gifts with retained income streams or reserve assets to maintain flexibility.

It is also important to recognize that probate avoidance does not necessarily mean the complete elimination of estate administration. Even with extensive lifetime gifting, some assets may remain in the individual's name at death, requiring probate. The goal is often reduction rather than total elimination. Lifetime gifts can shrink the probate estate to a manageable size, reducing costs and complexity even if probate cannot be avoided entirely.

From a practical standpoint, lifetime gifts are most effective when coordinated with other probate avoidance mechanisms. Joint ownership, beneficiary designations, and trusts all operate on the same fundamental principle of transferring ownership outside the probate process. Lifetime gifts complement these tools by proactively shifting assets during life rather than relying solely on arrangements that take effect at death. Together, these strategies can create a comprehensive plan that minimizes court involvement and maximizes efficiency.

The psychological dimension of lifetime gifting should not be overlooked. For many individuals, the act of giving during life provides satisfaction and reinforces family relationships. Seeing the benefits of the gift and the impact on recipients can be more meaningful than posthumous transfers. From an estate planning perspective, this emotional benefit aligns well with the practical advantage of probate avoidance.

Ultimately, the use of lifetime gifts to avoid probate reflects a shift in focus from death-centered planning to life-centered planning. Rather than viewing estate transfer as a single event occurring at death, lifetime gifting treats wealth transfer as a gradual, intentional process. Probate becomes less relevant because fewer assets remain to be transferred when death occurs. The legal system plays a smaller role, and personal planning plays a larger one.

Option 8: Ownership by Business Entities

One of the most effective and widely used approaches to avoiding probate is the ownership of assets through business entities. When structured properly, entity ownership changes the nature of what is transferred at death. Instead of transferring title to individual assets, the decedent transfers an ownership interest in an entity, or in some cases nothing transfers at all because ownership has already shifted by operation of law or contract.

At the most fundamental level, probate applies to assets owned in an individual's name at death. If an individual personally owns real estate, investment accounts, or operating businesses, those assets generally become part of the probate estate unless they are subject to a non-probate transfer mechanism. Business entities alter this result by interposing a legal owner between the individual and the underlying assets. The entity holds title, not the individual. The individual owns an interest in the entity, such as shares, membership units, or partnership interests. With careful planning, the transfer or continuation of that ownership interest can occur without probate.

Corporations provide one of the clearest illustrations of this principle. When an individual owns stock in a corporation, the corporation owns the business assets. The death of a shareholder does not affect title to corporate property. The corporation continues to own its bank accounts, real estate, intellectual property, and contracts without interruption. What potentially changes is the ownership of the shares. If those shares are held individually and pass under a will, they may still be subject to probate. However, if the shares are held in a revocable trust, transferred via a transfer-on-death registration where permitted, or governed by a buy-sell agreement requiring automatic redemption or purchase by surviving owners, the shares can pass without court involvement. In that case, probate is avoided even though the decedent's economic interest in the business is effectively transferred.

EXAMPLE

Robert Klein owned 40 percent of a closely held manufacturing corporation. The corporation itself owned the factory, equipment, patents, and operating accounts, all of which continued uninterrupted when Robert died. What changed was ownership of Robert's shares. Years earlier, Robert had placed his stock into a revocable living trust and signed a buy-sell agreement with the other shareholders. Under the agreement, the corporation was required to redeem his shares at death using life insurance proceeds. When Robert passed away, the trustee transferred the shares according to the agreement, and the corporation completed the redemption without probate. Robert's family received the cash value of his ownership interest, while the business continued operating seamlessly. The economic value changed hands, but no court was involved, and the corporation's assets were never at risk.

Limited liability companies are even more commonly used in modern estate planning because of their flexibility. An LLC can own virtually any type of asset, including operating businesses, rental real estate, marketable securities, and intellectual property. The individual owns membership interests rather than the assets themselves. Operating agreements can be drafted to specify what happens upon a member's death. Common provisions include the automatic transfer of economic rights to designated beneficiaries, continuation of management by surviving members or managers, and mandatory buyout of the deceased member's interest. If the membership interest is held by a trust or if the operating agreement itself effects a transfer on death, probate can be bypassed entirely.

The power of the LLC structure lies in the distinction between legal ownership and economic benefit. The entity continues uninterrupted, and the decedent's personal involvement may end without requiring judicial oversight. From the perspective of courts and title records, nothing changes. The LLC remains the owner of record. This continuity is especially valuable for real estate. Individually owned real property typically requires probate or ancillary probate in each state where property is located. By contrast, real estate held in an LLC does not change ownership at death. Only the membership interest changes, and that change can be handled privately under contractual arrangements.

EXAMPLE

Susan Patel owned three rental properties located in different states. Rather than holding title individually, she transferred each property into a single LLC of which she was the sole member. The LLC appeared on all deeds and leases as the owner, and Susan held only a membership interest. When Susan died, nothing changed in the public records. The LLC continued to own the properties, collect rent, and pay expenses without interruption. Susan's operating agreement directed that her membership interest pass to her children through her revocable trust. That transfer occurred privately, without probate in any state. Had Susan owned the properties individually, her heirs would have faced multiple probate proceedings. By using the LLC structure, she avoided court involvement while preserving the continuity of ownership and management.

Family limited partnerships function in a similar way and have long been used in estate planning for closely held assets. In a limited partnership, the partnership owns the assets, while family members own general and limited partnership interests. Partnership agreements often restrict transferability and provide for continuation upon the death of a partner. If a decedent's interest is structured to pass to heirs through a trust or to be acquired by remaining partners, probate can be avoided. In addition, partnerships and LLCs can centralize control, allowing senior family members to retain management authority while gradually shifting economic ownership to the next generation.

EXAMPLE

Harold Bennett owned a portfolio of farmland and commercial buildings and transferred them into a family limited partnership. Harold served as the general partner, retaining full control over leasing, financing, and sale decisions, while his two children held limited partnership interests. Over time, Harold gifted portions of the limited interests to the children, shifting economic value without surrendering management authority. The partnership agreement restricted transfers and required that, at death, Harold's remaining interest pass to a revocable trust for his heirs. When Harold later died, the partnership continued uninterrupted. Title to the properties never changed, and no probate court was involved. The children received Harold's partnership interest privately, while control mechanisms in the agreement preserved stability and prevented fragmentation of the family assets.

Trusts are often discussed as the primary probate avoidance tool, but business entities complement trusts rather than compete with them. In practice, trusts frequently own the entity interests, not the underlying assets. This layering enhances probate avoidance. The individual transfers assets into an LLC during life, then transfers the LLC interests into a revocable trust. Upon death, the trust becomes irrevocable and continues to own the entity interests. No probate is required because the trust, not the individual, owns the interests. The trustee administers the assets privately, guided by the trust agreement and the entity's governing documents.

EXAMPLE

Michael O'Connor owned several apartment buildings and a small logistics business. During his lifetime, he transferred each operating asset into separate LLCs, making the entities the legal owners of the real estate and business operations. Michael then transferred his LLC membership interests into his revocable living trust. While alive, he served as both trustee and managing member, retaining full control. At Michael's death, the trust became irrevocable, and his successor trustee automatically stepped in. The trustee continued to hold and manage the LLC interests according to the trust terms, distributing income to beneficiaries as directed. No probate was required because Michael no longer owned the assets or the LLC interests individually. The layered structure ensured continuity, privacy, and efficient administration without court involvement.

One of the less obvious but highly effective aspects of entity ownership is the role of contractual succession. Probate is fundamentally a judicial process triggered by death. Contracts, by contrast, operate independently of courts unless disputes arise. Operating agreements, shareholder agreements, and partnership agreements are contracts. They can specify exactly what happens when an owner dies. For example, a buy-sell agreement may require the entity or surviving owners to purchase the deceased owner's interest at a predetermined price or valuation formula. The purchase may be funded by life insurance, ensuring liquidity. When the agreement is properly drafted and implemented, the decedent's interest never becomes part of the probate estate in a meaningful way. The transaction occurs automatically, outside the court system.

EXAMPLE

David Morales was one of three equal owners of a consulting firm organized as an LLC. The operating agreement included a buy-sell provision requiring the LLC to purchase a deceased member's interest at fair market value, determined by a pre-agreed valuation formula. To fund the obligation, the LLC maintained life insurance policies on each owner. When David died unexpectedly, the insurer paid the policy proceeds directly to the LLC. Under the operating agreement, the LLC automatically redeemed David's membership interest using those funds. David's estate received the cash value of his ownership without delay, and the surviving owners continued the business without disruption. Because the transfer occurred by contract, not by court order, the process avoided probate while providing certainty, liquidity, and a clean transition of ownership.

This contractual approach also addresses one of the key risks of probate: the disruption of business operations. Probate can delay decision-making authority, freeze accounts, and introduce uncertainty at precisely the moment when continuity is most important. Entity ownership with clear succession provisions avoids this problem. Management authority can pass instantly to designated managers or remaining owners. Employees, customers, and lenders experience continuity rather than disruption. From a practical standpoint, this stability is often as important as the legal avoidance of probate itself.

Another important dimension is privacy. Entity ownership allows transfers to occur privately. Operating agreements and shareholder agreements are not filed with courts. Trusts are typically private documents. For individuals concerned about confidentiality, particularly business owners with sensitive financial information, avoiding probate through entity ownership preserves discretion.

Multi-state asset ownership further highlights the value of entities. An individual who owns property in multiple states may trigger probate proceedings in each jurisdiction. This ancillary probate multiplies costs and complexity. By consolidating ownership of those assets within a single entity, the individual transforms multiple potential probate proceedings into a single ownership interest. That interest can then be transferred without probate using trusts or contractual mechanisms. This strategy is especially common for investors with real estate portfolios spread across several states.

It is important to recognize that entity ownership does not automatically avoid probate. The effectiveness of the strategy depends on how the ownership interests themselves are held and transferred. If an individual owns LLC interests in their own name and leaves them to heirs under a will, probate may still be required. The key is aligning entity ownership with non-probate transfer mechanisms. This alignment is achieved through careful drafting, consistent titling, and ongoing maintenance. Estate planning failures often occur not because the structure is flawed, but because implementation is incomplete.

EXAMPLE

Karen Douglas formed an LLC to hold a valuable commercial property, believing this alone would avoid probate. She titled the property correctly in the LLC's name but kept her LLC membership interest in her individual name and relied on a simple will to pass it to her children. When Karen died, the property itself did not change ownership, but her membership interest became a probate asset. The executor was required to open probate to transfer that interest, delaying administration and increasing costs. Had Karen transferred her LLC interest into a revocable trust or used a permitted transfer-on-death designation, probate could have been avoided entirely. The entity structure worked as intended, but incomplete implementation undermined the result.

Tax considerations also intersect with probate avoidance planning, though they are conceptually distinct. Using entities to avoid probate does not eliminate estate taxes or income taxes. However, entities can facilitate tax planning strategies such as valuation discounts, income shifting, and orderly liquidation or continuation of businesses. While tax laws change over time, the fundamental probate avoidance benefit of entity ownership remains rooted in property law and contract law rather than tax law. This makes the strategy relatively durable.

Control is another subtle but critical advantage. Through entity governance provisions, owners can control who succeeds to economic benefits and under what conditions. Restrictions on transfer can prevent unintended heirs from becoming owners. Voting rights can be separated from economic rights. Management can remain centralized. These features are difficult or impossible to achieve through simple individual ownership combined with a will. By embedding succession rules in entity documents, owners reduce the likelihood of disputes that might otherwise draw assets into probate litigation.

EXAMPLE

Anthony Russo owned a multi-generation family business organized as an LLC. The operating agreement divided interests into voting and non-voting units. Anthony retained all voting units, giving him exclusive control over management decisions, while non-voting units carried the economic benefits. Over time, he transferred non-voting units to his children, but the agreement strictly limited transfers to spouses or outsiders. When Anthony died, the operating agreement required that his remaining voting units pass to a management trust controlled by a designated successor. The children received income distributions but could not interfere with operations or force a sale. Because succession rules were embedded in the LLC documents, ownership transitioned privately and predictably. The structure prevented disputes over control and avoided the risk of probate litigation disrupting the business.

For business owners, the psychological and operational benefits of certainty should not be underestimated. Knowing that ownership transitions are predetermined and legally enforceable reduces anxiety and allows for long-term planning. Heirs benefit as well. Instead of navigating probate courts, they receive interests or proceeds according to clear rules. This clarity often reduces family conflict, which is one of the most common and costly byproducts of probate.

There are also asset protection implications that, while separate from probate avoidance, reinforce the appeal of entity ownership. Assets held in entities may be insulated from personal creditors, subject to state law limitations. Although this protection is not absolute and must be respected in form and substance, it adds another layer of rationale for consolidating ownership within entities rather than holding assets individually.

Despite these advantages, entity-based probate avoidance requires discipline. Governing documents must be reviewed periodically to ensure that they reflect current intentions and comply with changing laws. Ownership records must be kept current. Beneficiary designations, trust provisions, and buy-sell agreements must be coordinated. Failure to do so can result in partial probate or unintended outcomes. In short, effective planning is holistic rather than piecemeal.

In sum, ownership by business entities transforms the probate question by changing what is owned at death and how ownership transitions occur. Instead of transferring title to individual assets through a public court process, the owner relies on private contracts and ongoing entities that survive death. Corporations, LLCs, and partnerships provide legal continuity. Trusts and contractual agreements provide transfer mechanisms. Together, these tools allow individuals to avoid probate in a lawful, predictable, and often elegant manner.

Option 9: Small Estate Procedures

Small estate procedures exist as a deliberate legislative response to the cost, delay, and formality of full probate administration. Probate is designed to provide court supervision over the transfer of property at death, protect creditors, and ensure that heirs receive what the law or a valid will entitles them to receive. For modest estates, however, the same procedural safeguards can become disproportionate to the value at stake. Filing fees, attorney costs, waiting periods, bond requirements, and ongoing court oversight can materially erode smaller estates, sometimes consuming a meaningful percentage of the assets themselves. Small estate procedures provide a streamlined alternative that preserves the core purposes of probate while reducing friction, expense, and delay.

At its core, a small estate procedure allows heirs or beneficiaries to collect and transfer a decedent's assets without opening a formal probate case. Instead of appointing a personal representative and navigating months or years of court-supervised administration, the law permits property to pass through simplified affidavits, declarations, or summary proceedings. These procedures are based on state law, and their availability, thresholds, and mechanics vary widely. Nevertheless, the underlying policy rationale is consistent across jurisdictions: when an estate falls below a statutory value threshold and presents minimal risk of dispute or creditor harm, formal probate is unnecessary.

One of the most common small estate mechanisms is the small estate affidavit. This document is typically executed by one or more heirs or beneficiaries after a waiting period following death. By signing the affidavit, the affiant attests under penalty of perjury that the decedent's estate qualifies as a small estate under state law, that the statutory waiting period has passed, that all known debts and expenses have been paid or will be paid, and that the affiant is entitled to receive the specified property. The affidavit is then presented to third parties such as banks, brokerage firms, or other asset custodians, who are authorized by statute to release assets in reliance on the affidavit without requiring probate court letters.

EXAMPLE

After Linda Foster died, her only significant assets were a checking account and a modest brokerage account, together well below her state's small estate threshold. Her daughter, Megan, waited the required 30 days and then completed a small estate affidavit. In the affidavit, Megan swore that Linda had no unpaid debts other than routine final expenses, that the statutory waiting period had passed, and that Megan was Linda's sole heir under state law. She signed the document under penalty of perjury and had it notarized. Megan presented the affidavit to the bank and brokerage firm, along with a death certificate. Relying on the statute, both institutions released the funds directly to Megan without requiring probate. The process avoided court filings, reduced costs, and allowed prompt settlement of Linda's affairs.

The practical effect of a small estate affidavit is to bypass the court entirely for certain categories of property. A bank holding a modest checking account does not need to see court appointment papers. The heir does not need to retain counsel or attend hearings. The transfer can occur within weeks rather than months. For families dealing with grief and immediate financial needs, this speed and simplicity can be invaluable. It also reflects a recognition that many estates consist primarily of liquid assets that pose little risk of complex administration.

Small estate procedures also extend beyond affidavits to summary administration or simplified probate. In these cases, a court filing may still occur, but the process is significantly abbreviated. Rather than a full probate with inventory filings, accountings, and prolonged creditor periods, the court may authorize distribution based on a simplified petition. Often, notice requirements are reduced, bond requirements are waived, and the court issues a single order transferring property. This approach strikes a balance between avoiding probate entirely and retaining minimal judicial oversight when appropriate.

EXAMPLE

When Harold Simmons died, his estate consisted of a paid-off condominium and a small savings account, together qualifying for his state's summary administration procedure. His niece, Claire, filed a simplified petition with the probate court requesting summary administration. Instead of preparing a detailed inventory and ongoing accountings, Claire submitted basic asset information and a death certificate. The court waived the bond requirement and reduced notice obligations because no disputes were anticipated and the estate value was modest. After a brief review, the judge issued a single order authorizing transfer of the condominium and release of the bank funds to Claire. The entire process was completed in a matter of weeks rather than months. The abbreviated procedure preserved limited court oversight while avoiding the cost, delay, and formality of a full probate proceeding.

The ability to avoid probate through small estate procedures depends heavily on the statutory definition of a "small estate." States typically set a dollar threshold based on the gross or net value of probate assets. Importantly, this valuation often excludes non-probate property such as jointly owned assets with rights of survivorship, payable-on-death accounts, transfer-on-death securities, retirement accounts with designated beneficiaries, and life insurance proceeds. Because these assets already pass outside probate, they are not counted toward the threshold in many jurisdictions. As a result, an estate that appears substantial at first glance may still qualify as a small estate for probate purposes.

This interaction between non-probate transfers and small estate procedures is critical. Estate planning techniques that minimize probate assets can make small estate procedures available even when overall wealth is moderate. For example, a decedent may have owned a home in joint tenancy, maintained beneficiary designations on financial accounts, and held only a modest personal checking account in their individual name. Although the decedent's total wealth may be significant, the probate estate may be small enough to qualify for simplified treatment. In this way, small estate procedures complement other probate avoidance strategies rather than operating in isolation.

EXAMPLE

When Evelyn Morgan died, her overall wealth was substantial, but very little of it required probate. Her home passed automatically to her spouse through joint tenancy. Her retirement accounts and life insurance proceeds transferred directly to named beneficiaries. Most of her savings were held in payable-on-death brokerage accounts. The only asset titled solely in Evelyn's name was a small personal checking account used for monthly expenses. Because nearly all assets passed outside probate, the remaining probate estate fell well below the state's small estate threshold. Evelyn's executor used a simplified small estate procedure to transfer the checking account with minimal court involvement. By coordinating beneficiary designations and joint ownership during life, Evelyn ensured that small estate rules applied at death. The strategies worked together, reducing delay and cost even though her overall estate was not small.

Another common small estate mechanism relates specifically to personal property. Some states allow heirs to collect tangible personal property, such as vehicles, household goods, or small personal effects, through affidavits or certificates of entitlement. Motor vehicle departments, for example, often have their own statutory procedures allowing title transfer based on a death certificate and affidavit when the vehicle's value falls below a certain amount. These targeted procedures further reduce the need for probate when the estate consists of discrete, easily identifiable assets.

From a creditor protection standpoint, small estate procedures typically preserve creditor rights while shifting responsibility to the heirs. Rather than relying on a court-supervised claims process, the law places the burden on the affiant or recipient to ensure that debts are satisfied. If creditors later emerge, they may pursue recovery from the assets or from the individuals who received them. Statutes often provide that recipients remain personally liable to the extent of the property received. This allocation of risk is a key policy tradeoff. The court steps back, but the law still provides remedies for unpaid creditors.

The avoidance of probate through small estate procedures also reduces administrative costs. Formal probate often requires professional assistance due to procedural complexity and fiduciary obligations. Even uncontested estates may incur thousands of dollars in legal fees and court costs. For small estates, these expenses can be disproportionate and unnecessary. By contrast, small estate affidavits are often prepared without legal assistance or with minimal guidance. Filing fees, if any, are modest. The net effect is a higher percentage of the estate reaching its intended recipients.

Timing is another significant advantage. Probate is inherently time-bound. Statutory notice periods, creditor claim windows, and court calendars impose minimum durations regardless of estate simplicity. Small estate procedures typically include a shorter waiting period following death, often ranging from a few weeks to a few months. Once that period expires, property can be transferred promptly. This can be particularly important when survivors need immediate access to funds to cover funeral expenses, housing costs, or other necessities.

Despite these advantages, small estate procedures are not without limitations. They are typically unavailable for real property[5], or available only under specific circumstances. Real estate ownership raises additional concerns related to title, liens, and creditor rights. Some states permit simplified transfer of real property through summary procedures or affidavits recorded in land records, but many require at least minimal court involvement. As a result, estates that include real property titled solely in the decedent's name may still require some form of probate, even if the property value is modest.

EXAMPLE

When Patricia Monroe died, her estate consisted mainly of a small house she owned outright and a modest checking account. Her son, Kevin, assumed he could use a small estate affidavit to transfer everything. While the bank released the checking account funds, the county recorder rejected the affidavit for the house. State law did not allow real property titled solely in the decedent's name to transfer by affidavit alone. Even though the home's value was below the small estate threshold, title concerns and potential creditor claims required court involvement. Kevin was forced to open a limited probate to obtain an order transferring the property. The process was simpler than full probate but still involved court filings and delays. The example illustrates that small estate procedures often fall short when real estate is involved, regardless of value.

Another limitation is the potential for disputes among heirs. Small estate procedures generally assume consensus or at least the absence of active conflict. If multiple heirs claim entitlement to the same property, or if the validity of a will is contested, simplified procedures may be inappropriate. Courts are reluctant to allow asset transfers without supervision when the risk of litigation is high. In such cases, formal probate provides a structured forum for resolving disputes and ensuring due process.

The existence of a will does not necessarily preclude the use of small estate procedures. In many jurisdictions, affidavits can be used whether the decedent died testate or intestate[6], provided the estate qualifies. The affidavit may incorporate the terms of the will and distribute assets accordingly. This flexibility allows small estates to honor testamentary intent without incurring the costs of probate. However, some states impose additional requirements when a will exists, such as filing the will with the court even if no probate is opened.

---

[5] Real property is land and anything permanently attached to it, such as buildings, improvements, and fixtures, together with the legal rights associated with ownership of the land.

[6] Testate describes a person who dies leaving a valid will that directs how their property is distributed, while intestate describes a person who dies without a valid will, causing state law to determine how their property is distributed.

> **Note:** From a practical standpoint, the success of small estate procedures depends on third-party compliance. Banks, financial institutions, and other custodians must be willing to accept affidavits and release assets. While statutes generally provide immunity to institutions that rely in good faith on a valid affidavit, risk-averse institutions may impose additional requirements or refuse to accept affidavits altogether. This can undermine the effectiveness of small estate laws in practice. Estate planners often advise clients to maintain clear beneficiary designations and minimize reliance on post-death affidavits for this reason.

Small estate procedures also serve an important access-to-justice function. Probate can be intimidating and inaccessible for individuals with limited legal knowledge or financial resources. Simplified procedures empower families to handle routine estate matters without professional intervention. This democratization of estate administration aligns with broader policy goals of reducing barriers to legal processes and ensuring that modest estates are not consumed by procedural overhead.

In the broader context of probate avoidance, small estate procedures occupy a distinct niche. They do not require advance planning, unlike trusts or lifetime transfers. They operate after death, responding to the circumstances as they exist rather than implementing a prearranged structure. This makes them particularly valuable for individuals who did not engage in formal estate planning or whose assets changed over time. In this sense, small estate laws function as a safety net, ensuring that even unplanned estates can be administered efficiently.

The interaction between small estate procedures and intestacy law is also significant. When a person dies without a will, small estate affidavits typically distribute property according to statutory intestacy rules. This ensures consistency with default inheritance policies while avoiding probate. However, intestacy distributions may not align with the decedent's informal wishes, highlighting the continued importance of basic estate planning even when small estate options exist.

From a risk management perspective, heirs using small estate procedures must be diligent. Because affidavits are executed under penalty of perjury, inaccuracies can expose the affiant to civil or criminal liability. Overstating entitlement, understating estate value, or ignoring known creditors can have serious consequences. This underscores that small estate procedures simplify administration but do not eliminate legal responsibility. The law substitutes personal accountability for court supervision.

EXAMPLE

After his aunt Eleanor died, Mark decided to use a small estate affidavit to collect her remaining assets. Wanting to move quickly, he stated in the affidavit that he was the sole heir and that all debts had been paid, even though he knew Eleanor had an outstanding credit card balance and a niece who might have a claim. The bank released the funds based on his sworn statement. Months later, the creditor and the niece challenged the transfer. Because Mark had signed under penalty of perjury, he was personally liable for the misstatements and faced both repayment demands and potential legal penalties. The simplified procedure spared court oversight, but it shifted responsibility squarely onto Mark.

In practice, small estate procedures often work best in conjunction with other probate avoidance tools. Beneficiary designations, joint ownership, and transfer-on-death arrangements reduce the size of the probate estate, increasing the likelihood that remaining assets qualify for simplified treatment. Together, these mechanisms can eliminate probate entirely or reduce it to a minimal formality. For modest estates, this integrated approach can achieve efficiency comparable to more complex planning structures at a fraction of the cost.

The broader societal impact of small estate procedures should not be overlooked. By reducing court caseloads and administrative burdens, these procedures allow judicial resources to be focused on larger or contested estates where oversight is genuinely needed. This efficiency benefits not only individual families but also the legal system as a whole. It reflects a calibrated approach to regulation, applying intensity where risk is high and restraint where it is low.

In summary, small estate procedures provide a pragmatic pathway to avoid probate for qualifying estates. Through affidavits, summary administration, and targeted transfer mechanisms, the law allows assets to pass quickly and inexpensively to heirs and beneficiaries. While these procedures are bounded by statutory thresholds and practical limitations, they play a critical role in modern estate administration. They acknowledge that one-size-fits-all probate is neither efficient nor equitable and that modest estates deserve proportionate treatment.

Option 10. Proper Titling and Coordination

For many families, the primary objective of estate planning is not to eliminate oversight entirely but to ensure that assets pass smoothly, privately, and with minimal delay. The proper titling of assets and coordination among ownership forms and beneficiary designations are among the most effective and underutilized tools for achieving that objective. When consistently applied, these techniques can significantly reduce or even eliminate the need for probate, regardless of whether a formal trust is used.

At its core, probate applies only to assets that are owned by the decedent individually at death and lack a contractual or statutory mechanism for automatic transfer. Assets that pass by operation of law or by beneficiary designation generally bypass probate entirely. Proper titling is therefore about aligning legal ownership with the intended method of transfer. Coordination ensures that these ownership structures work together, rather than at cross-purposes, and that they remain consistent as circumstances change.

One of the simplest ways to avoid probate is through joint ownership with rights of survivorship. When property is titled jointly in this manner, the surviving owner automatically becomes the sole owner at the death of the other, without court involvement. This is common with married couples who hold bank accounts or real estate as joint tenants with right of survivorship or as tenants by the entirety, where available. The legal effect is immediate and does not depend on a will. From a probate-avoidance standpoint, this can be highly effective, but it requires thoughtful application. Adding a joint owner is not merely a convenience. It is a present transfer of ownership rights, including potential exposure to the co-owner's creditors, divorce proceedings, or financial mismanagement. Proper titling in this context requires understanding that probate avoidance must be balanced against lifetime control and risk.

Beneficiary designations operate in a similar but more controlled manner. Retirement accounts, life insurance policies, annuities, and many financial accounts allow the owner to name one or more beneficiaries who will receive the asset upon death. These assets pass by contract rather than by will, and therefore do not enter probate. Proper titling here involves more than filling out a form. It requires precise beneficiary identification, the consideration of contingent beneficiaries, and periodic reviews. A designation that names a deceased individual, a minor without custodial provisions, or a former spouse can undermine the intended outcome and, in some cases, force probate or court intervention anyway. Coordination is critical because beneficiary designations override the terms of a will. An estate plan that leaves assets equally to children in a will but names only one child as beneficiary on a large retirement account will not achieve equality, regardless of the underlying intent.

Payable-on-death and transfer-on-death designations extend the beneficiary concept to non-retirement assets such as bank accounts, brokerage accounts, and even real estate in many jurisdictions. When properly titled with these designations, ownership remains entirely with the account holder during life, and the asset transfers automatically at death. This preserves control while avoiding probate. The effectiveness of these tools depends on careful coordination. If multiple accounts have different beneficiaries or percentages that are not aligned with the overall estate plan, the result may be confusion, unintended disparities, or liquidity problems for the estate. For example, if most liquid assets pass directly to beneficiaries while illiquid assets remain subject to probate, the estate may lack funds to pay debts or taxes, creating administrative complications that proper coordination could have prevented.

Trust ownership represents another powerful probate-avoidance strategy, but even here, titling is the operative mechanism. A trust does not avoid probate merely by existing. Assets must be retitled into the name of the trust, or otherwise made payable to it, to achieve the intended result. Proper titling ensures that legal ownership aligns with the trust structure so that, upon death, the trustee can administer and distribute assets without court involvement. Coordination is especially important when some assets are held in trust, others pass by beneficiary designation, and others are jointly owned. Each category must be evaluated for consistency with the overall plan. A common failure occurs when a trust is created but major assets remain titled individually. In such cases, probate may still be required, despite the presence of a well-drafted trust document.

EXAMPLE

Michael Reynolds created a revocable living trust to avoid probate and named his two children as equal beneficiaries. He transferred his brokerage account and savings account into the trust but never retitled his primary residence or updated the beneficiary designation on his retirement account. When Michael died, the successor trustee was able to distribute the trust-owned accounts immediately, without court involvement. However, the house was still titled solely in Michael's individual name, requiring a probate proceeding to transfer ownership. The retirement account passed directly to one child under an outdated beneficiary form, disrupting the intended equal split. Despite careful drafting, poor coordination undermined the plan. The trust worked as designed, but only for assets that were properly titled into it.

Real estate often presents the most visible probate issues, particularly when owned in multiple states. Proper titling can avoid ancillary probate by using joint ownership, transfer-on-death deeds, or trust ownership. Each method has different implications for control, taxation, and creditor exposure. Coordination is essential when real estate ownership interacts with other assets. For instance, transferring a residence into a trust may affect homestead protections[7], property tax exemptions, or mortgage terms if not handled correctly. Probate avoidance is not achieved simply by changing a deed; it requires integrating that change into the broader legal and financial context.

EXAMPLE

Linda Garcia owned a home in Arizona and a small vacation condo in Colorado. Wanting to avoid probate, she executed a transfer-on-death deed for the Colorado property but transferred her Arizona residence into her revocable living trust. After her death, her children recorded the transfer-on-death deed and avoided ancillary probate in Colorado. However, the Arizona home raised complications. The trust transfer had inadvertently disrupted a property tax exemption and required additional filings to preserve homestead protections. Although probate was avoided, the lack of coordination created administrative delays and unexpected costs. Linda's plan succeeded procedurally but exposed how real estate decisions cannot be made in isolation.

Coordination also involves aligning asset titling with incapacity planning. Many probate-avoidance tools serve dual purposes by facilitating management during a person's incapacity. Joint ownership may allow a co-owner to manage assets, but at the cost of diminished control. Powers of attorney provide authority without changing ownership, but they terminate at death, at which point titling determines whether probate is required. Trust ownership can provide continuity of management and avoid probate, but only if assets are properly transferred into the trust in advance. A coordinated approach ensures that the same structures that avoid probate also support

[7] Homestead protections are state-law rules that shield a primary residence from certain creditor claims, provide property tax benefits, and impose restrictions or formalities on how the home can be sold or transferred, particularly to protect the homeowner and surviving family members.

effective lifetime management, rather than creating gaps that require emergency court involvement.

EXAMPLE

Robert Chen planned carefully for incapacity and probate avoidance. He executed durable powers of attorney and created a revocable living trust, naming his daughter as the successor trustee. However, he delayed transferring several key assets into the trust, including a rental property and a large investment account. When Robert suffered a stroke, the power of attorney allowed his daughter to pay bills and manage daily finances, but the brokerage firm refused full authority over the untitled investment account. Court intervention was required to expand her authority. After Robert's death, the same assets triggered probate because they remained individually titled. The trust ultimately functioned as intended, but only for properly transferred assets. Earlier coordination would have avoided both the incapacity gap and probate exposure.

Another often overlooked aspect of coordination is tax planning. While probate avoidance is primarily an administrative concern, titling decisions can have tax consequences that indirectly affect the estate. Joint ownership may cause unintended gift tax issues or alter income tax basis adjustments at death. Beneficiary designations can concentrate tax-deferred assets in the hands of a single beneficiary, increasing that individual's tax burden. Trust ownership can provide flexibility in tax planning but only if assets are correctly titled and the trust terms are aligned with beneficiary designations. Proper coordination ensures that probate avoidance does not come at the expense of unnecessary tax costs or inequitable outcomes among heirs.

EXAMPLE

Thomas Miller named his oldest daughter, Karen, as the sole beneficiary of his IRA for convenience, assuming that she would share the proceeds with her siblings. At his death, the IRA passed directly to Karen outside of probate. Under the required distribution rules, she was obligated to withdraw the entire account within the applicable period, adding the distributions to her taxable income. The large withdrawals pushed her into a higher tax bracket and increased her Medicare premium surcharges. Meanwhile, her siblings received other assets that carried little or no immediate tax cost. Although the estate plan appeared equal on paper, concentrating tax-deferred assets in one beneficiary created a disproportionate tax burden and an unintended financial imbalance among the heirs.

Family dynamics further underscore the importance of careful titling and coordination. Adding a child as a joint owner to avoid probate may seem simple, but it can create perceptions of favoritism, expose the asset to that child's personal risks, and complicate equal distribution among siblings. Beneficiary designations can be structured to achieve clarity and fairness, but only if they are coordinated across all assets. When different assets pass through different mechanisms, the overall result should still reflect a coherent plan. Probate avoidance is not simply about speed or cost; it is about predictability and minimizing conflict at a time when families are already under stress.

The role of ongoing maintenance cannot be overstated. Asset titling is not a one-time exercise. Accounts are opened, closed, refinanced, or consolidated. Real estate is bought and sold. Beneficiaries marry, divorce, die, or fall out of favor. Each change creates an opportunity for misalignment. Proper coordination requires periodic review to ensure that titling and beneficiary designations continue to reflect current intentions and integrate with the rest of the estate plan. Many probate proceedings arise not because planning was never done, but because it was not updated.

Even with meticulous planning, some assets may still require probate, and in some cases, a limited probate is unavoidable or even desirable. The goal of proper titling and coordination is not necessarily to eliminate probate at all costs, but to control its scope and impact. When the majority of assets pass outside probate, any remaining court process is typically faster, less expensive, and less contentious. This outcome reflects successful coordination, where probate becomes a backstop rather than the primary mechanism of transfer.

In practice, effective probate avoidance through titling and coordination depends on understanding how different legal mechanisms interact. A will does not retitle assets. Beneficiary designations supersede wills. Joint ownership transfers property immediately at death. Trusts require funding. Each rule is straightforward in isolation, but complexity arises when they intersect. Proper coordination brings these elements into alignment so that each asset follows a clear and intentional path at death.

Ultimately, probate avoidance is achieved not through any single document or technique, but through the consistent application of ownership principles across the entire balance sheet of a household. Proper titling determines how assets move. Coordination ensures that they move together, in the intended direction, without unnecessary friction. When these principles are applied thoughtfully, families benefit from reduced administrative burden, enhanced privacy, faster access to assets, and a smoother transition during one of life's most difficult periods.

Summary

This course explained how probate can be reduced or avoided through intentional ownership and beneficiary structures. It emphasized that probate avoidance is achieved through titling and contractual mechanisms, not through wills alone, and that tools such as trusts, joint ownership, beneficiary designations, and transfer-on-death arrangements must be properly implemented to be effective. Throughout the course, the focus remained on coordination, demonstrating how incomplete or inconsistent planning can still trigger probate despite the best intentions. The overarching lesson is that probate avoidance is a structural outcome that depends on aligning legal ownership, lifetime control, and post-death transfer mechanisms into a coherent plan.

Glossary

B

Beneficiary designation. A contractual instruction naming who will receive a specific asset at death outside of probate.

I

Incapacity planning. The use of legal tools to manage assets and decision-making if a person becomes unable to act for themselves.

J

Joint ownership with right of survivorship. A form of ownership where the surviving owner automatically receives full title upon the death of the other owner.

P

Payable-on-death account. A financial account that transfers directly to a named beneficiary upon the owner's death.

Pour-over will. A will that directs any assets left outside a trust at death to be transferred into the trust through probate.

Probate. The court-supervised legal process used to validate a will, settle debts, and transfer ownership of a decedent's assets.

Probate estate. All property owned solely by a decedent at death that does not transfer automatically by contract or operation of law.

R

Revocable living trust. A trust created during life that holds title to assets and allows for private administration and distribution without probate.

T

Tenancy by the entirety. A survivorship ownership form available to married couples that often provides additional creditor protection.

Transfer-on-death deed. A recorded deed that transfers real estate to a named beneficiary upon the owner's death without probate.

Transfer-on-death registration. A designation that allows securities or accounts to pass automatically to a beneficiary at death.

Index